... Down with the wig
  And the mask of the prig!
  Do what they can
  To smooth and conceal it,
  They're forced to reveal it—
  He was a *man!*...

By Robert Haven Schauffler, from the
poem, "Washington." Courtesy of
the Schauffler Estate.

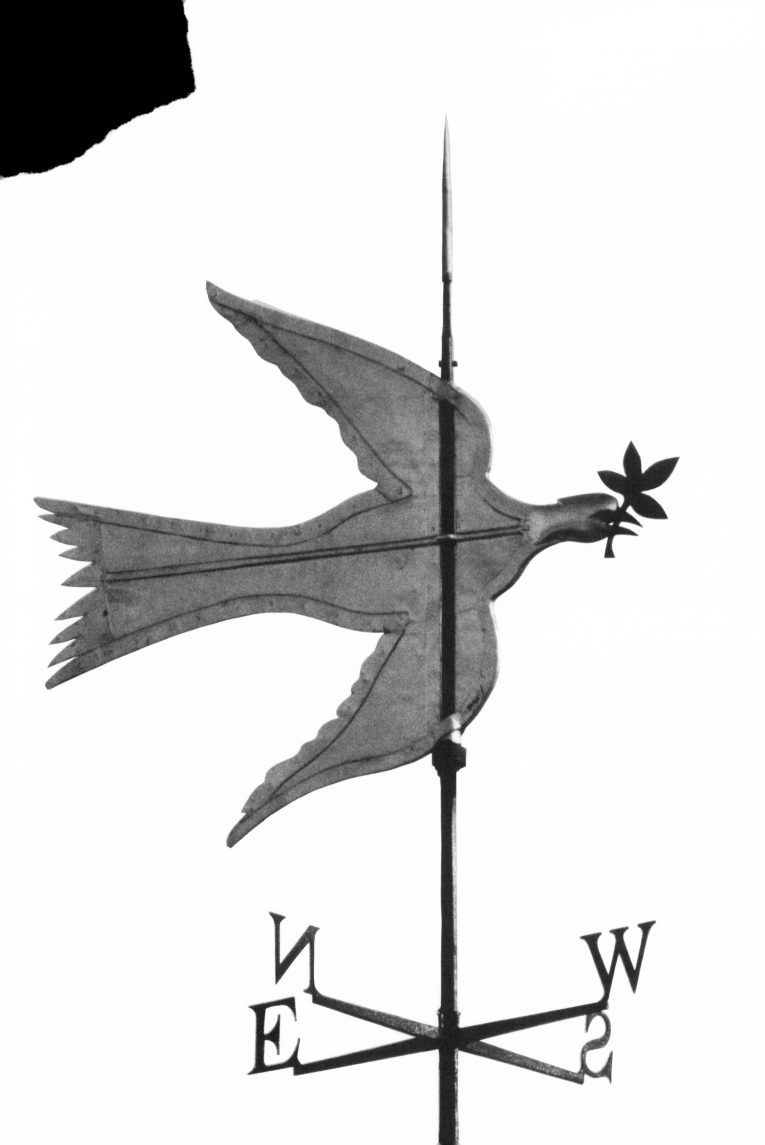

RIDER WITH DESTINY

GEORGE WASHINGTON

BY LONNELLE AIKMAN

LINK PRESS, PUBLISHERS

McLEAN, VIRGINIA

1983

Manufactured in the United States of America

First edition

Designer: Gerard A. Valerio
Editor: Nancy Link Powars
Picture Editor: Geraldine Linder

COVER:

Portrait by John Trumbull, an aide to General Washington during the Revolution, and an artist who knew and painted many of its leaders from life. *Courtesy, The Henry Francis du Pont Winterthur Museum.*

BINDING:

Washington family coat of arms.

ENDPAPERS:

Front: George Washington Birthplace at Wakefield, Virginia.
Engraving by J. Duthie after Chapman. New York Public Library

Back: Family Tomb at Mount Vernon, Virginia.
Engraving by W. H. Capone after W. H. Brooke, *History of the United States of America* by Col. T. P. Schaffner, 1863

FRONTISPIECE:

Mount Vernon's famous weather vane—a dove of peace bearing a green olive branch in its beak.
Courtesy Mount Vernon Ladies' Association of the Union

LIBRARY OF CONGRESS CATALOGING IN PUBLICATION DATA

Aikman, Lonnelle.
　　Rider with destiny: George Washington

　　Bibliography: p.
　　Includes index.
　　1. Washington, George, 1732-1799. 2. Washington, George, 1732-1799
—Homes—Virginia—Fairfax County. 3. Washington (D.C.)—History.
4. Mount Vernon (Va. : Estate) 5. Presidents—United States—
Biography.
　　I. Title.
E312.A54　　　　1983　　　　973.4′1′0924　　　　[B]　　　　83-11983
ISBN 0-912991-00-3 (hardbound)
ISBN 0-912991-01-1 (paperback)

Contents

Foreword

GEORGE WASHINGTON was the only American president who lived his entire life in the eighteenth century. This may help explain why he has so consistently frustrated biographers who try to peer into his private character and reveal facts that will make him seem more familiar to us. For though the eighteenth century saw the beginnings of modern democracy in America and France, it remained a time of rigid class structures and behavior patterns. Aristocrats were expected to shoulder many public burdens. They also enjoyed the privilege of privacy. We cannot name the favorite menus nor count the peccadillos of, say, Lord Cornwallis, so why should we expect to become intimate with his adversary, a Virginia aristocrat with the same sense of duty and privilege?

Yet we do expect it. Democracy, growing as a concept as well as a political device, soon made Americans feel they had the right to unravel the mysteries of Washington. Even today we feel an honest need to find warm blood beneath the cold marble of this monumental hero. And because American writers have found so little about the man to titillate their readers, they have resorted to every device from the rather charming mythology of Parson Weems to the recent cynicism which has presented our hero as a mincing boor or a cold-eyed profiteer.

Whatever titillation lurks in George Washington's background will not be easily wrested from his eighteenth-century defenses. His privacy stands firm, and in these pages there is no assault upon it. Instead, the man is shown in terms we can be sure of—first the facts of his life, then in the context of the building of his city (an extraordinary story), finally in the environment he loved best, Mount Vernon.

And magically, the character of our hero emerges. Here is the small boy who drew animals and birds in the margins of his copybook; the adventurous and quick-learning youth; the vigorous and immensely vital soldier; the statesman whose resources of patience and conciliation were as vast as his vision. Finally, here is the host and *pater familias*. He greeted an endless parade of guests with unbounded cordiality, treated them with charm and gentle humor, got the young people to dancing and then tactfully withdrew if they seemed overwhelmed by his presence.

Without mining for new secrets about Washington, but simply by tracing his path through a fascinating array of known facts, these pages produce the man with a fullness of character that has been sought so often before. It is a pleasure to meet him.

EDWARDS PARK

February 22, 1983

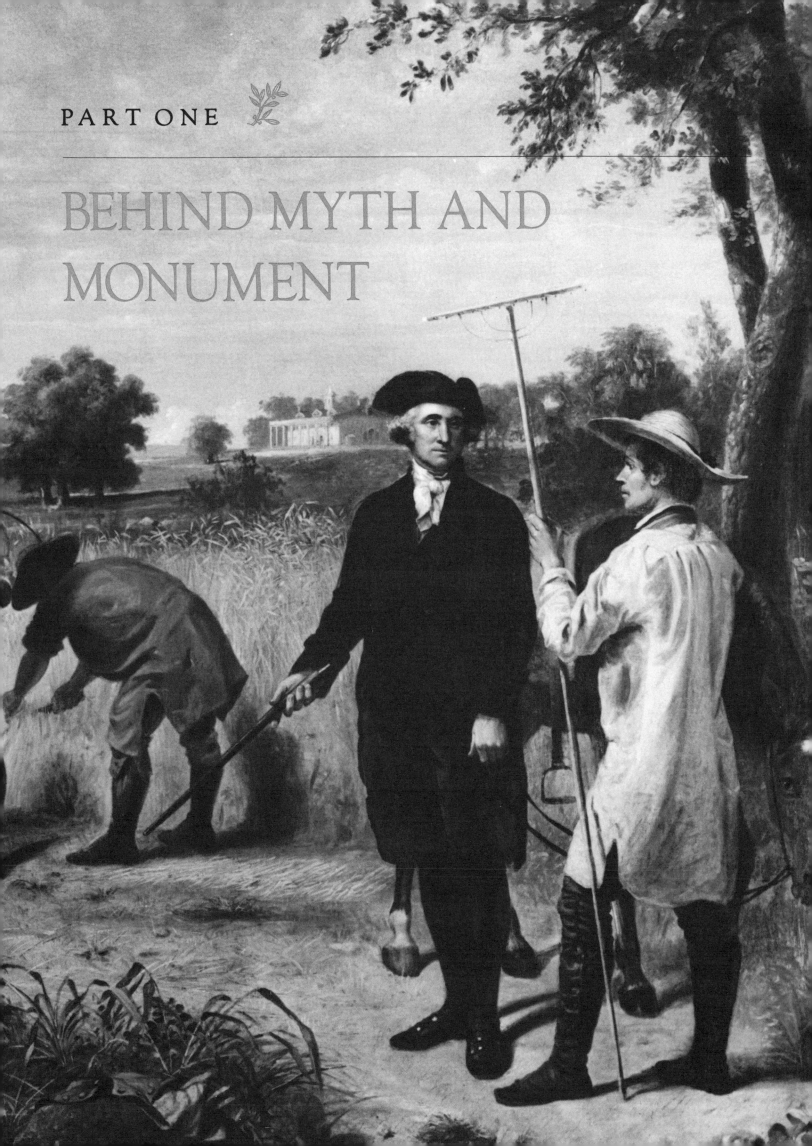

PART ONE

BEHIND MYTH AND MONUMENT

CHAPTER 1

Growing Up in the Colonies

S OON AFTER THE PARIS PEACE TREATY, the jubilant victors of the American Revolution told a story of the toast made by Benjamin Franklin in honor of his old friend and colleague, George Washington.

Dr. Franklin was then serving as United States Minister to the French court. At a dinner held in Versailles, according to a fellow guest, the British Ambassador had proposed a toast to England as the "Sun" whose rays nourish the earth. The French Ambassador followed with another to France as the "Moon" whose steady beams cheer nations in their dark hours.

Finally, the new Republic's elder statesman and philosopher-scientist stood up, glass in hand, "To George Washington," he said, "who like Joshua of old commanded the sun and moon to stand still, and they obeyed him."

Most Americans still recall with something like awe the achievements of their Revolutionary leader and first President. Popular writers have poured out millions of words about him—and produced a legendary personality as stiffly noble as the marble statues generations of admirers have raised to him.

Flying across the United States today, you are seldom far from one of the hundreds of towns, cities, counties, rivers, lakes, and mountains named by grateful citizens for the Father of their Country.

Few sizable communities lack a Washington Street or Square, a Washington Hotel, Bank, or other business concern. Hardly a schoolhouse or city hall is without its steel engraving of his austere countenance.

In the Nation's Capital that bears Washington's name stands the tallest and, some think, the most impressive memorial ever erected to a hero. More than 555 feet high, the Washington National Monument soars above the city's low skyline with a simplicity that denies the fascinatingly complex character of the man. Yet there is a region where you can look behind the frozen image of success and find the young Washington—warm, human, striving.

It is a green and smiling land. Still largely given to farming, it rolls for mile after mile across Tidewater Virginia, south of the winding shores of the lower

PRECEDING SPREAD:

To cultivate the land, Washington once wrote a friend, "has been my favorite amusement." In this painting, the master of Mount Vernon is pictured indulging in the art at one of his five farms. Washington's methods in soil conservation, crop rotation, and experimental farm machinery were advanced for the time, and carrying out his projects was a labor of love into which he flung himself whenever he was free of the public duties that so frequently claimed his attention and energy.

Painting by Junius Brutus Stearns. Courtesy The Virginia Museum of Fine Arts

OPPOSITE:

Washington's Birthplace at Wakefield, Virginia, recalls rural scenes familiar to the boy. At this site, a National Monument since 1930, visitors see a "Memorial House" furnished with articles representing a typical middle-class dwelling of the time. Recent excavations, however, have revealed the much larger foundations of the house in which George was actually born, and which burned down in 1779.

Engraving by J. Duthie after Chapman, New York Public Library

Potomac River. Within this once plantation-dotted countryside, Washington was born and came to manhood. Here you can visit his Wakefield birthplace, now a National Monument, and stop at Ferry Farm, now privately owned, where he spent his boyhood. Here you can wander about his restored Mount Vernon home, his "own Vine and Fig Tree" by the Potomac, to which he returned with joy after each adventure for his country.

Amid scenes such as Washington knew, it is intriguing to trace the pattern of events—sometimes called destiny—that brought a modest country gentleman to leadership in the birth of a nation.

Riding, swimming, and hunting on family plantations toughened the boy for frontier and wartime hardships he would meet. Growing up in open country, fatherless from the age of 11, he developed traits of self-reliance and initiative that run like strong bright threads all through his life.

As a youthful surveyor, Washington glimpsed a continent's sweep that stretched his horizons and gave roots to his faith in free men's right to their own land. As a British-Colonial officer in the French and Indian War, he learned guerrilla tactics that would help defeat George III's Redcoats. As a Virginia legislator, he discovered political arts that would come in handy to a general coaxing military funds from Congress's meager budget.

Indeed, many of Washington's experiences seem curiously fated. Time and again he emerged unscathed from disease and battle in which others about him lost their lives.

One of the strangest of these narrow escapes occurred just before the Revolutionary battle of Brandywine Creek. The General and a companion were riding horseback near the stream when they were spotted by one of Lord Cornwallis's officers—a crack shot—concealed in nearby woods. Failing to recognize his quarry, the Britisher stepped forward shouting, and aimed his weapon. Washington stopped briefly, then "slowly cantered away," as the officer later told the story. "It was not pleasant," he explained his forbearance, "to fire at the back of an unoffending individual who was acquitting himself very coolly of his duty."

The man who would be "first in war, first in peace, and first in the hearts of his countrymen" began life February 22, 1732, a fourth generation British-American and a member of Virginia's landed gentry.

These were useful assets. They admitted George Washington automatically to the close-knit plantation society whose wealthy, influential leaders could make or break a colonial career.

Behind the infant stretched also a long line of well-born, well-educated forebears. Lawrence Washington, last of George's paternal ancestors to remain in England, was a prosperous Anglican rector and a Fellow of Brasenose College at Oxford University.

Ironically, this great-great grandfather of America's Number One Rebel was labeled a "malignant Royalist" and stripped of his parish during Parliament's revolt against Charles I in the 1640's. But the family disaster wove another strand in fate's web. It drove Lawrence's son John to a seagoing career that ended in shipwreck on the shores of the Potomac.

Arriving about 1656 in Virginia's "Northern Neck" between the Potomac and Rappahannock Rivers, John Washington married a wealthy planter's daughter. Backed by Ann Pope's 700-acre dowry farm, he embarked on the colonists' favorite enterprise—accumulating land grants.

From then on, the Washington clan multiplied and prospered. Though never among the great landowners, they gradually amassed large, valuable properties. When George came into the world as the eldest son of Augustine and his second wife, Mary Ball, it was on a 2,500-acre estate, later called Wakefield, overlooking the Potomac between Pope's and Bridges Creeks.

That year Benjamin Franklin celebrated his 26th birthday and began publishing *Poor Richard's Almanack*. It was three years before the birth of John Adams, who would follow Washington as second President of the United States. And 11 years before, a red-haired baby boy named Thomas Jefferson—future author of the Declaration of Independence and third American President—would open his eyes on another Virginia estate known as Shadwell.

Driving today on Historyland Highway (Virginia Route 3), you come to a sign some 40 miles southeast of Fredericksburg. The sign tells you that you are approaching the National Monument that was Washington's birthplace. Two more miles by country road, you reach a simple granite shaft. Beyond lies the eighteenth century.

Here, at what is now called Wakefield, is a peaceful, bucolic setting of colonial buildings and gardens. And here, it is pleasant to recall, the toddler George spent his beginning years.

His earliest memories must have been of vistas, such as those we see today, of wide green lawns and pastures, framed by parklike woods, rolling down to the still waters of Pope's Creek.

At this farm, long before George was born, the Washington family established itself firmly in America. Within the family cemetery, with its worn seventeenth- and early eighteenth-century gravestones, rest 32 Washingtons—including George's great-grandfather John, his grandfather Lawrence, and his father Augustine. Buried here, too, was Augustine's first wife, Jane Butler Washington, who died in 1728 of one of the swift, mysterious ailments that filled the pioneers' graveyards.

The house by Pope's Creek in which George was born burned down in 1779. Near its site stands a sturdy brick building of eighteenth-century design. It was built by the Wakefield National Memorial Association and presented to the United States Government in 1932 to embellish the Birthplace National Monument.

Since no information on the original dwelling was then available, the

OPPOSITE:
Mary Ball Washington, pictured at Ferry Farm with her son George, was once described as the "presiding genius of her household, commanding and being obeyed." She was overpowering enough, apparently, to keep George from accepting an early offer of a seafaring career, thus altering future American history.

Illustration by Alonzo Chappel. *Life and Times of Washington,* by John Frederick Schroeder

Memorial House represents simply a typical, middle-class Tidewater home of the period.

Little George may have been taken to such homes in the neighborhood, to perch on chairs and play with toys like those now on view in the Memorial House. But his own home, we now know, was far from typical. According to the latest archeological digs conducted in the 1970's by the National Park Service, his birthplace was a much larger, basically brick building, with at least nine rooms. Surrounding the main structure were its service outbuildings, its vegetable and herb gardens, and a sizable colonial farm.

Within this privileged environment, a small boy would certainly have delighted in the farm animals that abounded, and in the exciting spectacle of wild ducks and geese flying in to rest on the plantation's creek shores and marshy lands.

The Pope's Creek idyll ended, however, in 1735. When George was nearly four years old, his father moved the family up the Potomac River to a farm on Little Hunting Creek that would some day be world famous as Mount Vernon.

By then George had a sister and brother, Betty and Samuel. He had looked on the face of grief at the death of his 13-year-old half sister Jane. And he had yet to meet his half brothers Lawrence and Augustine, who, before he was born, had been sent away to school in England, as were youngsters of some of the more affluent colonial families.

At his isolated Hunting Creek home, the elder Washington created another self-sustaining farm. He was elected to the vestry of Truro Parish. And he fathered two more children, John Augustine and Charles.

But George's father was too enterprising to pass up a business opportunity that developed with the discovery of iron on his Accokeek Creek property near the young village of Fredericksburg. Soon after Charles's birth in 1738, he moved again, this time to Ferry Farm, on the Rappahannock River opposite Fredericksburg. There George gained another sister, named Mildred, though she survived for little more than a year.

A new world of people opened up to George at his third home in a short lifetime. There was the wonder of living near his first settlement, and the fun of riding the shuttling ferry that gave the farm its name.

Some of America's favorite folklore has grown up around the boy's normal outdoor life at Ferry Farm. Across the Rappahannock, in the familiar anecdote, he hurled a stone, a silver dollar, or a Spanish piece of eight to show off his muscle.

And who has not heard how young George chopped down his father's favorite cherry tree, and couldn't tell a lie about it?

That fanciful tale grew out of one published in the 1806 edition of a popular biography, *The Life and Memorable Actions of George Washington.* It was written by a jolly traveling parson called Mason Weems, who was also an itinerant book salesman, and a best-selling author whose own lively tracts were sweetened to the moralizing taste of the times.

"Run to my arms, you dearest boy," Weems had Augustine Washington say to his son. "Glad am I, George, that you killed my tree . . . Truth is . . . an act of heroism . . . more worth than a thousand trees, though blossomed with silver, and their fruits of purest gold."

Such colorful legends are recalled today as part of Fredericksburg's annual celebration of Washington's birthday. February 22, 1982—the 250th anniversary of his birth—offered a high point for this festive occasion. Among other events, the city put on a costume party at the restored home of his mother, Mary Ball Washington, while Masonic Lodge No. 4 held a special ceremony in honor of their famous member who first joined the Masonic Order at Frederickburg on November 4, 1752.

Growing up at Ferry Farm, the boy Washington met one of his most painful and formative experiences. There, in 1743, his father's death ended the first happy, carefree period of his young life.

Word of Augustine Washington's illness had brought George hurrying home from a visit with relatives at Chotank on the Potomac. The next day, his father—49 years old and a giant of proverbial strength—was dead of what was then called "Gout of the Stomach."

For five more years George spent part of his time with his mother at Ferry Farm, while making long visits with his half brother Augustine back at Wakefield, and with Lawrence at Mount Vernon. It was at this time, too, that George, restrained by his mother's stern discipline, gave up a chance to go to sea, thus changing the course of American history.

"Whoever has seen that awe-inspiring air and manner so characteristic in the Father of the Country," one of the lad's playmates later wrote, "will remember the matron as . . . the presiding genius of her well-ordered household, commanding and being obeyed."

But George had his own will and fire. Breaking in a wild colt, he once rode the rearing, plunging beast with such stubborn force that it was said to have collapsed and died under him. When his mother asked about her valued horse, according to the legend, young Washington again won praise by admitting the truth.

While at Ferry Farm, George received most of his formal education. It covered "reading, writing and accounts," said one report, "taught by a convict servant whom his father brought over [from England] for a school master."

Such tutors were common, and the boy may well have had one. But there is evidence he also attended a Fredericksburg school.

In surviving notes and copy books written in a round childish hand and adorned with marginal birds and animals, we find hints of studies that included elementary geography, Latin, and English composition. There are exercises in geometry, "a very useful and Necessary Branch of the Mathematick," and copies of legal forms used then for wills and land and business deals.

The most famous samples of George's instruction are the 110 "Rules of Civility and Decent Behavior in Company and Conversation." Copied by him

when he was about 14, the original text can still be seen at the Library of Congress in Washington, D.C.

"Kill no Vermin as Fleas, lice tics &c in the Sight of Others," said one maxim that throws interesting light on the problems of practicing gentility at the time.

"Cleanse not your teeth," advised another, "with the Table Cloth Napkin, or Knife."

There were warnings not to "play the Physician" when visiting the sick, against sleeping in company, mocking the serious, and showing joy at another's mishap.

"In Pulling off your Hat to Persons of Distinction," the proper young man was admonished, "make a Reverence, bowing . . . according to the Custom of the Better Bred." As for inferiors, "those of high Degree ought to treat them with affibility & Courtesie, without Arrogancy."

In short, the boy's Rules of Civility reflect a crystal-ball image of the grown man's tact and good sense. In the same way, Washington's integrity can be seen as a general projection of his boyishly misspelled maxim: "Labour to keep alive in your Breast that Little Spark of Cetial [celestial] fire called Conscience."

The boy Washington (right) rides with his beloved half brother Lawrence over the Mount Vernon estate when it was owned by the older son. George was in love with this Potomac-side property from the beginning, but he acquired it in 1754 only at the cost of deep sorrow over his brother's untimely death.

District of Columbia Public Library, Washingtoniana Division

CHAPTER 2

Adventures as a Young Man

OPPOSITE:

Venturing into the open country to the west, Washington continues his training toward becoming an accomplished surveyor. Working with characteristic care and enthusiasm, he produced surveys that were accurate and complete.

The Pictorial Life of George Washington by John Frost

MATURITY CAME EARLY to George even in an age when hard reality soon turned adolescents into adults.

Finding his father's old surveying instruments, the boy made practical use of the science of "Mathematick" that already enchanted him.

Before he was 16, he had mastered simple drafting and surveying methods, and was earning cash or its equivalent in tobacco. One of his first tasks was to measure a turnip field for his half brother Lawrence, who had married in 1743 and settled down on his inherited estate at Little Hunting Creek on the Potomac.

As the family's eldest son, Lawrence took a paternal interest in George. And George, 14 years younger, hero-worshipped a brother who not only had acquired the polish of an English education, but the glamor of having fought in a foreign war.

In 1741 Lawrence had served as an officer in the British siege of Spain's Caribbean port of Cartagena. The campaign ended in disaster, though with no blame attached either to Lawrence or his commanding officer, Admiral Edward Vernon. And, in fact, Captain Washington later named his Hunting Creek place "Mount Vernon" in the Admiral's honor.

After he was 16, George lived at Mount Vernon. There he became part of the gilded circle of planters' aristocracy that his half brother had achieved by propinquity and marriage.

Lawrence's wife, Anne Fairfax, was the daughter of rich Colonel William Fairfax, who owned the nearby plantation of Belvoir. In turn, the Colonel was cousin and often host to Thomas, Lord Fairfax, proprietor of millions of acres of New World land.

With beginner's zest, George learned the fashionable games of whist, loo, and billiards. He trained his huge hands to hold tiny teacups, his oversized feet to step to the minuet and Virginia Reel. He grew familiar with talk of philosophy, the classics, and the latest English novels, such as Henry Fielding's *Tom Jones*. Taking part in romantic amateur theatricals, he developed a lasting passion for drama.

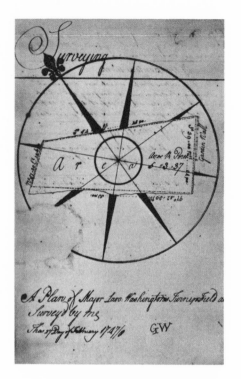

As a beginning surveyor, Washington was only 15 years old when he made this drawing of a turnip field belonging to his half brother Lawrence.

Library of Congress

While still too young to wed, George also discovered the thrill of flirting and the pangs of rejection by junior misses whose only claims to fame rest on their hapless pursuit by the then-obscure youth.

Inspired by blissful agonies of unrequited love, George composed mournful verse "for her that's Pityless of my grief. . . ."

He bewailed his shyness in an acrostic dedicated to "Frances Alexa"—probably the daughter of a neighboring Alexander family.

"Ah! Woe's me, that I should Love and conceal," he began the A line. "Long have I wish'd," went L, "but never dare reveal."

In lugubrious letters to his friends, we read of a mysterious "Low Land Beauty," who has spurned his "chast and troublesome Passion." And smile in sympathy to find that in his despair he was torn between living "more retired from young Women," or seeking solace in the company of "a very agreeable Young Lady" he had recently met.

More serious than these meteoric fancies was the long and hopeless attachment that George apparently conceived in early Mount Vernon days for Sally Fairfax, wife of his friend and neighbor, young George William Fairfax.

From letters found after Sally's death, scholars have argued for and against the possibility that Washington's obvious fascination ever flamed into acknowledged love. Perhaps, some surmise, the bittersweet ordeal was the beginning of the iron self-discipline for which Washington was noted.

Certainly, the letters reveal that he was deeply influenced by the charming, witty girl who would become mistress of Belvoir after her husband inherited it from his father, the Colonel. Sally, too, may have enjoyed his youthful devotion and was not above a bit of coquettish teasing.

Nearly half a century after that first springtime (and well after his own successful marriage), Washington wrote the widowed Mrs. Fairfax that all the great events since could not erase "the recollection of those happy moments, the happiest in my life, which I have enjoyed in your company."

The ambitious young surveyor had better luck in his career. Fox-hunting with Lord Fairfax, who often visited Belvoir, George won the old man's heart by his bold horsemanship and modest bearing. When Fairfax sent out a surveying party, in March 1748, to mark tenant farms on his vast Shenandoah Valley holdings, George Washington went along for the experience.

The trip was worth more than money to the lad. Riding down the Valley in Virginia's fragrantly budding spring, he first sensed what beauty—and profits—awaited settlers beyond the mountains.

". . . we went through the most beautiful Groves of Sugar Trees," he wrote in his faithfully kept journal, "down ye river [to] Land exceeding Rich and Fertile. . . ."

"Not being so good a Woodsman as ye rest," George confessed to his diary, he was given a bed in one frontier cabin.

*Washington dances a minuet
with alluring, unattainable
Sally Fairfax, wife of his
friend and neighbor, George
William Fairfax.*

District of Columbia Public Library,
Washingtoniana Division

To his "Surprize," he found it "nothing but a Little Straw—Matted together without Sheets or any thing else but with Double its Weight of Vermin. . . ." He quickly joined his comrades by the fire.

But Mount Vernon's sheltered 16-year-old soon learned to camp out, to do his share of the work, and to help with surveying despite rains and sometimes flooded rivers.

A highlight of the trip for George was a sudden encounter with some 30 Indians returning from the warpath with a trophy scalp.

"We had some Liquor with us of which we gave them Part," he explained, "it elevating there Spirits put them in y. Humour of Dancing. . . ."

The braves built "a great Fire," formed a circle, and listened to a long harangue by their chief. Then, in George's words, "y. best Dauncer jumps up as one awakened out of a Sleep and runs and Jumps about y. Ring in a most comical manner . . . Musick," he added, "is a Pot half [full] of Water with a Deerskin Stretched over it . . . and a goard with some Shott in it to Rattle."

The grotesque spectacle of savages whooping and cavorting against the flickering firelight seemed "comical" then to a novice in the wilds. But Washington had received an elementary lesson in the red man's customs and weakness for the white man's firewater.

The following year, after qualifying for the job at Virginia's capital of Williamsburg, he obtained a lucrative post as county surveyor. Thereafter, on frequent western trips, he steadily added to his knowledge of the frontier and its inhabitants.

He saved his money, invested it in nearly fifteen hundred acres of land in and around the Shenandoah Valley, and generally appeared on his way to becoming a solid subject of the British Empire.

Meantime, a family crisis interrupted the young man's pursuit of fortune, and sent him on his first and only ocean journey.

As fall breezes warned of summer's end in 1751, Lawrence Washington's long, nagging illness became worse. His symptoms spelled tuberculosis, for which doctors advised a milder climate. Since Lawrence's wife was kept at home by their fourth and only surviving child, George accompanied his half brother to Barbados, Britain's tropical West Indies isle.

From the start, the flight to health was doomed, though a Barbados doctor who examined Lawrence cheerfully promised a cure.

Family connections brought the brothers a flood of invitations, including one from a typical English club "call'd the Beefstake and tripe," as recorded in George's Barbados diary.

With a farmer's eye, the younger Washington observed "fields of Cain, Corn, Fruit Trees." He had never seen so many fruits at the table, he wrote breathlessly: "Granadella the Sappadilla Pomgranate Sweet Orange Water Lemmon forbidden Fruit apples Guavas, &ca. &ca. &ca."

He wondered how a people so favored "shou'd be in debt," a situation he discovered by diligent questioning, and blamed on high interest charges for land loans.

"Dined at the Fort with some Ladys," he reported, but he did not let their "very agreeable" company distract him from learning the precise gun-power of the "pretty strongly fortifyed" base.

The inquiring young man also sampled the theater, being "treated with a play ticket" to the popular *Tragedy of George Barnwell*. The plot dealt with a merchant's apprentice lured by a woman into theft and murder. It was a lively tale, and the performance was perhaps the first professional one that George had ever seen. But no one would have guessed it from his cautious diary comment. "The character of Barnwell and several others," he wrote, "was said to be well perform'd."

Yet for all the hospitality and warm, relaxing air of Barbados, Lawrence grew no better. He decided to move on to Bermuda, while George returned to Mount Vernon with letters and news for the family.

When Bermuda also failed Lawrence, he finally came home to die, in midsummer of 1752. The loss was a hard blow for George, though it meant that within a few years—following the remarriage of Lawrence's widow and the death of their last child—he would come into his precious Mount Vernon.

As for the futile Barbados trip, George gained more from it than information on fruits and forts. He had caught smallpox there, recovered, and thenceforth would be immune. The disease left its mark on his handsome young face, but a few pits were small price for lifetime protection against this often fatal affliction.

Was it fate again? A quarter-century later, when smallpox decimated his troops in winter camps, General Washington was spared to carry on the Revolution.

CHAPTER 3

Preparation for a Rebel

THE BOY WHO HAD LISTENED, enthralled, to Lawrence Washington's adventures in the Cartagena campaign naturally came to yearn for military glory of his own.

Soon after his half brother's death, George applied to Governor Robert Dinwiddie for the post Lawrence had held—and earlier recommended him for—Virginia's Militia Adjutant.

The Governor and his Council felt that the job was not only too big for young Washington, but had grown too much for any one man. So four District Adjutancies were created, of which George, just before his 21st birthday, received one.

He was lucky to get it, with a major's rank and pay, in spite of criticism of his youth and inexperience. Moreover—call it coincidence, perhaps—he began his military career at a most auspicious time. The long rivalry between Britain and France for the North American continent was about to erupt into its last phase—the French and Indian War.

Like checkers on a gigantic board, French trading posts and forts stretched along the St. Lawrence River to the Great Lakes, and down the Mississippi to New Orleans. The British held the Eastern Seaboard as far as the Alleghenies, and had pushed on beyond where land-grant speculators engaged in fur trade and settlement projects.

Prominent among such groups was the Ohio Company of Virginia, in which many of Virginia's leading families, including the Washingtons, held shares. And it was toward the Company grant, in the vast Ohio River basin, that the French moved south in 1753, threatening British America.

Governor Dinwiddie decided to send a message to the French field commander, demanding withdrawal. Major Washington volunteered for the duty. He left Williamsburg just as autumn leaves portended winter rigors in rougher country than he had yet seen.

Washington's small party included the able frontiersman and guide, Christopher Gist, two traders, two "Servitors," and a French-speaking interpreter. Besides arms, food for men and horses, and medicines, they carried

OPPOSITE:
As a major in the Virginia militia, Washington leads a hazardous, 500-mile mission into the wild region of the Ohio River basin. His orders were to demand the withdrawal of French forces from Fort LeBoeuf, a base from which they were threatening British interests in the region. Washington's meeting with the French field commander, the Chevalier de St. Pierre, brought a defiant reply and opened the way to the French and Indian War.

Engraving from painting by Alonzo Chappel. *Life and Times of Washington* by John Frederick Schroeder

A prowling Indian warrior shoots at Washington—and misses—during the return trip of the British expedition from the French Fort LeBoeuf.

People's History of the United States by John Clark Ridpath

OPPOSITE:
George Washington, portrayed by Charles Willson Peale as a regimental colonel of Virginia troops during the French and Indian War. While still in his twenties, he had already survived several perilous incidents in what some would call a "providential" destiny.

Engraving by J. W. Steel. New York Public Library

wampum belts and gifts for the Indians. The Major's orders were to deliver his message, bring back an answer, report on French strength, and woo Indians to the British side.

It was quite a mission for one not yet 22.

The party's objective was Fort LeBoeuf, near Lake Erie, across 500 hazardous miles. Along the way, Washington heard disturbing reports of French plans—at one point even from French officers. Having "dosed themselves pretty plentifully [with wine]," Washington wrote in his notebook, "They told me, That it was their absolute Design to take possession of the Ohio, and by G—they would do it."

En route, the Major also learned much in parleys with wary tribal chiefs. One, called Half King because his power was shared with others, was more friendly to the English. He and his men accompanied the group on the trip's last lap.

At Fort LeBoeuf, the French commandant, the Chevalier de St. Pierre, received the visitors politely. He agreed to transmit Dinwiddie's letter to his superiors, but made it clear, as he said in his written reply, that France would "contest the Pretentions of the King of Great Britain."

Even as he entertained the envoys, St. Pierre was trying to persuade their Indian escort to join the French. He used, Washington observed, "every Stratagem which the most fruitful Brain could invent."

But Washington won in the end. The Indian chief left with the Virginians as they began the long, hard journey home. And, finally, Washington reached Williamsburg safely on January 16, 1754, after two narrow brushes with death.

Washington escapes drowning—with the aid of frontier-guide Gist—in the freezing waters of the Allegheny River. This incident was his second close call during the return trip from Fort LeBoeuf. Was it another example of the charmed life attributed to America's future hero?

Sketch by William Ranney. Claude J. Ranney, Malvern, Pennsylvania

One occurred when a prowling Indian shot at him and Gist after they had left the others to make a short cut through the woods. The assailant was "not 15 steps off, but fortunately missed," Washington wrote later. "We took this Fellow into Custody . . . Then let him go and walked all the remaining Part of the Night."

Washington's other close call came in crossing the partly-frozen Allegheny River on an improvised raft. "Before we were Half Way over," he reported, "we were jammed in the Ice." He tried to stop the raft with his pole "that the Ice might pass by . . . it jerked me out into ten Feet Water but I fortunately saved myself by catching hold of one of the Raft Logs."

The news of French operations on the frontier made Washington a celebrity overnight. Governor Dinwiddie was so impressed by the Major's report on French plans and arms that he rushed it into print for attention in London as well as in the Colonies.

When spring came, Washington was commissioned a regimental lieutenant-colonel, and sent out with Virginia troops to support a fort going up at the strategic Forks of the Ohio, where the Monongahela and Allegheny Rivers meet. He was on his way when he learned that the French had taken the fort without resistance.

Still undeclared was a New World struggle known in America as the

After his defeat at Fort Necessity (an improvised shelter
hastily erected at Great Meadows, Pennsylvania), Washington signs his capitulation to
the French and Indian victors.
The blow was softened, however, by an agreement whereby
Washington and other sur-
vivors were permitted to leave
the fort as free men, and to
retain small arms for protection from hostile Indians on
the long trek home.

Illustration by F. O. C. Darley. *Our
Country* by Benson J. Lossing

French and Indian War, and in Europe as the Seven Years War. Colonel Washington fired what is reported to have been its opening shot on May 28, 1754, when he attacked a force of some 30 Frenchmen encamped in hiding near his advanced base, southeast of the Ohio Forks.

The French commander, the Sieur of Jumonville, and nine of his men were slain—thereby sparking an international controversy not yet resolved: Jumonville's captured papers could be read two ways. He was either an enemy spy, or a friendly ambassador, as the French later insisted.

Washington, however, had no doubts. Calling the group "Spyes of the worst order," he sent his prisoners on to Williamsburg and prepared to meet certain reprisal. He made his stand on Great Meadows at a hastily erected shelter he called Fort Necessity. It might equally well have been named Fort Misery.

As the French army and its Indian allies advanced, Washington's Indian supporters (more than a thousand) slipped away. Soon he and his few hundred men were surrounded by Frenchmen and whooping Indians. Amid the din of shooting and yelling, torrential rains fell.

The beleaguered garrison fought in the open, behind earthworks, and in the flooded trenches, as the attackers, in Washington's words, "from every little rising, tree, stump, Stone, and bush kept up a constant galding fire upon us."

After nearly ten hours, it was the French who sought a parley. Washington agreed to surrender under terms that permitted the defenders to march out as free men, drums beating, with "honors of war." The survivors were even allowed to keep small arms to shoot game and to protect them from Indian scalpers on the grim road home.

At Williamsburg, people were shocked at the British catastrophe, though they praised Washington for courage against heavy odds. His reputation was spreading, too. After the Jumonville victory, he had written his younger brother, John Augustine, "I heard the bullets whistle, and, believe me, there is something charming in the sound."

The letter was published in the *London Magazine*, and quoted to George II, who remarked that the young man would not think them so charming if he had heard many.

By then, Washington's disenchantment with whistling bullets had already begun at Fort Necessity. His next campaign rammed the point home.

In the spring of 1755, another British army headed west to retake the Ohio Forks and its fort, now named Duquesne, from which the French dominated the frontier.

Commander-in-chief was His Majesty's General Edward Braddock, dispatched from England with two regiments of regular troops to drive the French out for once and all.

George Washington accompanied the General as a staff aide, an honorable though unpaid post he accepted gladly as a chance to serve with an outstanding Royal officer.

Supply and transport problems, however, plagued the expedition. Illness forced Washington himself to fall behind. Cured by Doctor James's powders, "the most excellent medicine in the world," he said, he was still "very weak and low," when he caught up with the troops near Fort Duquesne.

The battle broke on July 9 the day after his arrival, when the British vanguard, clearing a path through the woods, suddenly came on a band of French and Indians. British fire scored first. Then the French dispersed their men behind trees and bushes surrounding Braddock's long exposed lines.

As the Indians' shrieks split the air, the fight turned into a rout. The confused British soldiers, trapped between the hidden foe and their own officers flogging them on, clawed one another to escape.

General Braddock was mortally wounded. Most of his officers were killed or maimed. But Washington was unharmed.

"I now exist . . . in the land of the living by the miraculous care of Providence," he wrote to John Augustine after the battle. "I had 4 Bullets through my Coat and 2 Horses shot under me. . . ."

When Fort Duquesne finally fell in 1758, Washington again was there.

In the three-year interim between Britain's disastrous and successful campaigns, he had commanded Virginia's whole chain of border forts protecting

settlers from Indian raids. He was constantly in the saddle, checking military terrain, recruiting and training men, pleading for supplies—in fact, gaining priceless experience for the future Revolution against George III.

But the real key to frontier peace in the 1750's, the young officer felt, was to oust French and Indian allies from the Ohio Forks base. London agreed and in 1758 ordered General John Forbes and his regulars to make another try.

This time it was Colonel Washington, with his own Virginia regiment. And once more his curious luck held. It was November, wet and cold, before his army laboriously reached within a day's ride of the fort. Its exhausted leaders were about to postpone the attack until spring when Washington, on a foray from camp, captured three prisoners. As he later wrote, they "providentially fell into our hands."

Learning from them that the French were desperately weak, the British troops pushed on. But let Washington end the story:

"I have the pleasure to inform you," he reported to Virginia's new Governor, Francis Fauquier, "that Fort Duquesne, or the ground rather on which it stood, was possessed by his Majesty's troops on the 25th instant. The enemy . . . burned the fort, and ran away [by the light of it] at night."

With the Ohio region secured, the British high command would carry the struggle for the continent north to a decisive victory in 1759, on the embattled Plains of Abraham above Quebec.

Washington said farewell to arms, forever he thought. He turned to his waiting Mount Vernon farm, to politics, and to marriage.

British General Edward Braddock is buried with military ceremony after suffering mortal wounds during his disastrous campaign to take Fort Duquesne from French and Indian defenders. The grave was dug under a traveled road, a site so chosen to prevent marauding Indians from desecrating it. Here Washington reads the funeral service.

Engraving by J. Rogers after J. McNevin. *Washington, a Biography* by Benson J. Lossing

OVERLEAF:
At the last British-French confrontation at Fort Duquesne on the Ohio Forks (where Pittsburgh now stands), Washington salutes the raising of the British flag of victory.

Engraving by T. B. Smith after J. R. Chapin. *Washington, a Biography* by Benson J. Lossing

Marriage and Domestic Peace

A RICH YOUNG WIDOW also was waiting. Just when and how Washington met and wooed Martha Dandridge Custis is lost in clouds of romantic hearsay. As a sociable young man invited to the great houses of the Virginia Colony, he may have known her when she was happily married to Daniel Parke Custis, owner of White House Plantation on the Pamunkey River near Williamsburg.

Certainly the evidence shows that George and Martha were acquainted by March 1758—nearly a year after her husband's death—and that shortly they were engaged.

It was a practical and promising union. At 27, sweet-tempered, house-wifely Martha needed a husband to manage Custis's large estate left to her and their children, John and Martha, or "Jackie" and "Patsy."

Washington's integrity and good business sense made him just the man. Moreover, Colonel Washington was not only handsome and famous; he was fond of children, and ready to take little Jackie and Patsy to his heart along with their mother.

The wedding was held January 6, 1759, soon after Washington's return from the finally successful Duquesne campaign and his resignation from the army.

Though details have been lost, the Church of England ceremony and the reception at the bride's "White House" were clearly brilliant affairs, attended by leading state and military dignitaries.

The bride, guests recalled, wore silver-brocaded white silk, looped over a quilted petticoat, pearls in her hair, sparkling buckles on satin shoes. Her tall bridegroom appeared in civilian blue cloth, scarlet lined, with gold shoe-and-knee buckles, a dress sword at his side.

"Many of the grandest gentlemen, in their gold lace, were at the wedding," an ancient servant would tell Martha's grandson, George Washington Parke Custis, three-quarters of a century later. "But none looked like the man himself!"

OPPOSITE:
Handsome Colonel Washington woos a charming and wealthy widow, Martha Dandridge Custis, at her inherited estate on the Pamunkey River near Williamsburg. Playing at her feet are her two children, Martha Parke (Patsy) Custis, and John (Jackie) Custis.

Engraving by G. R. Hall after painting by J. W. Ehninger. New York Public Library

The honeymoon coincided with Washington's new career as a Burgess of the Virginia Assembly at Williamsburg.

Ironically, it seems now, he had lost out twice (1755 and 1757) for the office in the Colony's legislative house. Success came at the Frederick County election of July 1758. Though he had been too busy preparing for the Duquesne expedition to campaign personally, his name led those of all candidates.

Actually, Washington was never an active vote seeker. His most revealing effort was made, not in his own behalf, but for his friend and neighbor, George Fairfax, husband of lovely, unattainable Sally.

While arguing for Fairfax at Alexandria in 1755, Washington had infuriated a bantam-sized opponent named William Payne. Seizing his stout hickory cane, Payne knocked the towering colonel to the ground.

Washington, unhurt, restrained his indignant friends and returned to his quarters. After thinking it over, he sent a note to Payne requesting a meeting at a convenient tavern. The little man appeared, braced for a dueling challenge.

Instead, his adversary met him, hand extended, with an apology for the offending remark.

Washington first took his seat in the Virginia Assembly on February 22, 1759—his 27th birthday. He was "straight as an Indian," a fellow member described him, "measuring 6 feet 2 inches in his stockings, and weighing 175 lbs. . . . A pleasing and benevolent tho a commanding countenance, dark brown hair which he wears in a cue [queue] . . . His demeanor at all times composed." That composure was badly shaken when the House unanimously adopted a resolution thanking Washington "for his faithful Services to his Majesty and this Colony." The blushing young Burgess stood up, as colleagues told the story, but was too embarassed to speak.

"Sit down, Mr. Washington," said the Speaker. "Your modesty is equal to your valor, and that surpasses the power of any language that I possess."

Peace and domesticity would smooth the next fifteen years of Washington's life.

As soon as he could wind up his immediate Assembly duties in the spring of '59, he gathered together his bride, stepchildren, and assorted family trunks and boxes, and hurried on to Mount Vernon.

Along the road he sent a message ahead to his manager. "You must have the House very well clean'd," he said, "and were you to make Fires in the Rooms below it w'd Air them . . . get two of the best Bedsteads put up . . . Enquire abt in the neighborhood and get some Egg's and Chickens. . . ."

At long-neglected Mount Vernon, its master found "terrible management and disadvantages," he wrote a friend. "I had provisions of all kinds to buy . . . Buildings to make, and other matters, which swallowed . . . all the money I got by Marriage."

In Virginia's House of Burgesses, Washington attended his first session as a member on February 22, 1759, about a month after his wedding. From then on, Burgess Washington played an increasingly active role in pre-Revolution events, as Virginia joined other colonies in opposing restrictive British rule. The building depicted here by Howard Pyle is the one in which Washington served, not the version that visitors see today in restored Colonial Williamsburg. That building is a reconstruction of the still earlier House that burned down in 1742.

Painting by Howard Pyle. *Harper's Monthly Magazine,* May 1896

Back at Mount Vernon in the spring of 1759, Washington becomes a country squire at the head of his new family— Martha and his stepchildren. "I am now, I believe, fixed at this Seat with an agreeable Consort for Life," Washington wrote a friend in cheerful ignorance of events to come.

Illustration by Alonzo Chappel. *Life and Times of Washington* by John Frederick Schroeder

Gradually, however, Washington organized his farm into a self-contained manorial estate, producing fine tobacco and wheat.

Up with the sun, he plunged into "the life of a Husbandman," which "of all others," he declared, "is the most delectable."

As a family man denied children of his own, Washington gave a father's love to Martha's Jackie and Patsy. His concern shines through long lists of items ordered from London: "For Master Custis, 6 yrs. old, A Coach and six in a box," and "6 pockt Handf, small and fine." Or "For Miss Custis, 4 . . . 2 Caps, 2 pr. Ruffles, 2 Tuckers, Bibs, and Aprons, if fashionable."

The Washingtons entertained lavishly and were often invited to neighboring plantations. They were invited to balls and races at Annapolis. They shared in Williamsburg's glittering social life during annual sessions of the Assembly, to which Washington was reelected from 1760 to 1772.

They also kept a town house and held a pew at Christ Church in Alexandria, Fairfax County seat. As a young surveyor, Washington had helped lay out this settlement. Later he would serve there as a county judge on both civil and criminal cases.

These were busy years for the Squire of Mount Vernon. The cheerful routine of personal affairs was interrupted only in 1773 by grief over the death of Mrs. Washington's daughter Patsy (Martha Parke Custis). Long a sufferer from epileptic seizures, she was only 17 when she died.

Like his father, George Washington became a vestryman of Truro Parish. On his way from Williamsburg to attend sessions of the House of Burgesses, he would visit his mother while she was still at Ferry Farm, and afterward at her Fredericksburg house that he had bought for her in 1772. He also stopped frequently to see his married sister, Betty Washington Lewis, at the Lewis's Fredericksburg home—now restored and exhibited to the public as Kenmore. And as he passed through town, he doubtless called on old friends of the Fredericksburg Masonic Lodge, which he had joined in 1752.

In addition, Washington even made periodic inspection trips to his early investment properties in the Shenandoah region, and checked on the Custis holdings around Williamsburg.

Yet with all his activities, Washington never forgot the greener fields beyond the mountains. In 1770 he retraced his first trip into the wild Ohio country to claim free land that the Assembly had voted veterans of the French and Indian War.

Traveling by horseback and canoe with his small party, Washington shot buffalo, renewed acquaintance with Indian chiefs, eager now for trade with the English—and kept a sharp lookout for fertile, watered tracts.

Out of this expedition Washington eventually gained, by grant and purchase, more than 20,000 acres of valuable frontier land. With his other possessions, he was a rich man—in real estate at least—with power and influence in his community.

But there was a cloud over his and his friends' seemingly sunlit future. In the distance, a thoughtful man could hear the sound of muskets and the rumble of drums.

The storm that exploded into the American Revolution was gathering darkly by the early 1770's. Colonial leaders, including Washington, increasingly resented British taxes, trade restraints, and, above all, the attitude that the mother country knew best how to treat her overseas offspring.

"The Parliament of Great Britain hath no more right to put their hands into my pocket, without my consent," Washington wrote a British apologist in 1774, "than I have to put my hands into yours for money."

Burgess Washington was no abstract philosopher like young Thomas Jefferson, fellow Assembly member and brilliant graduate of William and Mary College. "In action cool, like a Bishop at his Prayers," he was more prudent than Patrick Henry, who had warned as early as the 1765 Stamp Act that "Caesar had his Brutus, Charles I his Cromwell, and George III—may profit by their example."

Colonists fight British soldiers to keep their Liberty Pole. Such tall poles, raised here and there during the turbulent years before the final break with England, gave evidence of increasing independence and rebellion.

Illustration by F. O. C. Darley. Our Country by Benson J. Lossing

OPPOSITE:

Virginia delegates, including Washington, Patrick Henry, and Richard Henry Lee, meet with other colonial representatives in Philadelphia for the first Continental Congress of 1774. Washington, standing outside Carpenter's Hall, wears his colonel's uniform from the French and Indian War. He would wear the uniform again at the second Continental Congress in 1775, when he was elected Commander-in-Chief to lead the American Army against the British.

Painting by Clyde O. DeLand. Historical Society of Pennsylvania

But Washington prophetically predicted that "more blood will be spilt . . . if the ministry . . . push matters to extremity, than history has ever yet furnished instances of in the annals of North America." And he supported the resistance all the way.

He joined the colonial effort to curtail imports from England, thus "starving their Trade and manufactures," as he put it in a letter to George Mason, a like-minded neighbor at Gunston Hall.

He attended the outlawed Assembly meeting in May 1774, at Williamsburg's Raleigh Tavern, where the Burgesses urged the Colonies to write against British coercion.

He served as one of the Virginia delegates to the first Continental Congress held soon after in Philadelphia and again at the second one called on May 10, 1775.

Meantime, military events were fast overtaking all civil action. At Lexington and Concord, undeclared war had flared on April 19, 1775, when "the embattled farmers stood and fired the shot heard round the world."

Then on the same May day that the Second Continental Congress met, a cocky Vermonter named Ethan Allen seized Britain's sleeping Fort Ticonderoga on Lake Champlain. According to his own account, Allen took this action "in the name of the Great Jehovah and The Continental Congress."

A month later on June 15, 1775, the Second Continental Congress unanimously elected George Washington to lead the American armies against the British Empire.

CHAPTER 5

Through Revolution's Blood and Tears

The NEW COMMANDER-IN-CHIEF broke the news to his Martha, anxiously waiting at Mount Vernon, in a letter starting "My Dearest . . ."

"I assure you . . . " he wrote, "I have used every endeavor . . . to avoid it . . . and that I should enjoy more real happiness in one month with you at home, than I have the most distant prospect of finding abroad, if my stay were to be seven times seven years."

As it happened, it was indeed seven years and more before Washington was home again, though Martha made long and arduous journeys to join him in winter quarters between every campaign.

"I am imbarked on a wide Ocean, boundless in its prospect," he wrote brother John Augustine in 1775, "and from whence perhaps no safe harbour is to be found."

Washington faced his first test at British-held Boston, after taking command of his Continental Army at Cambridge on July 3, 1775.

For eight months neither side moved. The rebels, numbering some 20,000 men, needed artillery and training. The British general, Sir William Howe, with fewer troops, was in no hurry to clash again with militia marksmen. On June 17 he had led a bloody assault up nearby Breed's Hill and suffered a costly victory against Colonials holding their fire till they could see the whites of the enemies' eyes.

It was not until a March morning in 1776 that Boston's 12,000 Redcoats awoke to find Washington dug in at Dorchester Heights, with cannon trained on town and harbor. Howe was forced to sail for Nova Scotia with his remaining troops and Tory friends. Anchoring at Halifax, he awaited help to push the war in earnest.

Looking back on the struggle through the glow of success, it is easy to forget how uncertain and difficult it was then for amateurs—farmers, carpenters, and villagers—to fight Britain's professional armies and navies.

The Americans met defeat after defeat on Howe's return with vastly increased military and naval strength. Washington gave up Long Island, New

OPPOSITE:
Yankee Minutemen and British troops exchange fire in the opening skirmish of the Revolution at Lexington, Massachusetts. ". . . if they mean to have a war," the American leader, Captain John Parker, is reputed to have declared, "let it begin here!"

Engraving from painting by Alonzo Chappel. New York Public Library

OVERLEAF:
In taking command of the American Army on July 3, 1775, Washington is pictured here as if surrounded by welcoming officers and men. Actually, the new general arrived without announcement in Cambridge, Massachusetts, to find a ragtag collection of soldiers lacking discipline or adequate equipment.

Illustration by Alonzo Chappel. *Life and Times of Washington* by John Frederick Schroeder

A Congressional committee, made up of Benjamin Franklin, Thomas Lynch, and Benjamin Harrison, visits Washington at Cambridge in October 1775. They have come to gather information on the deplorable state of Washington's army, and to report back on methods by which more men and money can be obtained from the colonies.

Illustration by B. West Clinedinst. *The Story of the Revolution* by Henry Cabot Lodge

On January 1, 1776, General Washington raises the flag of the "United Colonies" over Prospect Hill near Boston. Its 13 red and white stripes represented the 13 colonies in revolt against the Crown, but the emblem was misunderstood by the King and his American sympathizers because it retained the red field of the Union Jack. Washington soon cleared up the seeming gesture of appeasement—verbally by pungent comments, and practically by continuing the siege of British-held Boston.

Painting by Clyde O. DeLand

From Dorchester Heights, overlooking the city and harbor of Boston, Washington forces the evacuation of occupying troops under the British General, Sir William Howe. In this bloodless victory of March 1776, Washington gained the advantage by throwing up overnight fortifications and supporting them with impressive lines of cannon that had been dragged by ox-train across snow and ice from Fort Ticonderoga.

Painting by H. Hintermeister. Courtesy Fraunces Tavern Museum, Sons of the Revolution, New York

Temporarily in control of New York City, Washington and his troops listen—on July 9, 1776—to an official reading of the recently passed Declaration of Independence. Though not everyone realizes the timing, the bloody struggle to cut ties with England was already well underway in both northern and southern colonies before the divided Members of Congress finally agreed on July 4 to pledge their lives, fortunes, and "sacred Honor" to the cause.

Painting by H. Hintermeister. Courtesy Fraunces Tavern Museum, Sons of the Revolution, New York

Fired by the announcement of the Declaration of Independence, New York patriots celebrate by toppling the statue of George III from its pedestal on Bowling Green. The monument's lead pieces were turned into Rebel bullets, but the city itself would be captured by the British in less than two months.

Life of George Washington by J. T. Headley. New York Public Library

After his overwhelming defeat in the Battle of Long Island on August 27, 1776, Washington calls a council of war with his generals. The unanimous decision was to evacuate the American Army to save it. The meeting itself was held in Brooklyn, New York, at the home of Philip Livingston, who had served in the First and Second Continental Congresses, and who signed the Declaration of Independence.

Painting by John Ward Dunsmore. Title Guarantee and Trust Company, New York

With the British holding Manhattan, Long Island, and the surrounding country, Washington leads the retreat across New Jersey through November chill, rain, and mud. His strategy, it has become clear, is to save his small and battered army to fight another time.

Illustration by W. Croome. *Pictorial History of the United States* by John Frost

York, White Plains, and Fort Washington; then slowly retreated across New Jersey into Pennsylvania.

By mid-December he was discouraged enough to write that without "the speedy enlistment of a new army . . . I think the game will be pretty near up."

Yet with typical tenacity, he gathered his forces on Christmas day 1776, crossed the Delaware, and surprised the relaxed Hessian mercenaries at Trenton.

He captured nearly a thousand prisoners, to his own "trifling" loss, as he reported to Congress—"only two Officers and one or two privates wounded."

Thus war's chart went up and down. Washington won the Battle of Princeton; lost at Brandywine Creek to General Howe. As British troops marched into Philadelphia, Congress fled to temporary capitals carrying its brave Declaration of Independence.

The surrender of Britain's General Burgoyne to General Horatio Gates at Saratoga, in October 1777, gave a great lift to the American cause. Then, two months later, Washington's ragged troops were freezing and starving at Valley Forge. Amid snowfields stained with the blood of barefoot soldiers, some 3,000 died of exposure, "camp fevers," and smallpox.

Washington, however, held firm. "I have no doubt . . . we shall triumph over all our misfortunes," he wrote a new volunteer officer, the young Marquis de Lafayette of France.

Washington's prophecy was soon reinforced when he received the welcome news, in April 1778, that the French were officially joining in the war against England. Eventually, France would contribute money, ships, and thousands of fighting troops.

The survivors of Valley Forge emerged toughened and trained as never

On the bitter-cold Christmas night of 1776, Washington directs the ferrying operation that transports his weakened army across the Delaware River from Pennsylvania to New Jersey. The maneuver, carried out in secret, permitted him to surprise and overwhelm Britain's mercenary Hessians at Trenton, where they were celebrating the holidays by drinking and carousing.

Engraving by J. N. Gimbrede after painting by Thomas Sully

A freezing, starving, and ailing army endures the rigors of winter in 1777-78 at Valley Forge, Pennsylvania. Yet out of this ordeal of suffering and death, Washington's troops would emerge as a strong, disciplined force, thanks to the skill of a Prussian drillmaster, General-Baron von Steuben, who had volunteered to serve in the American Revolution.

Painting by F. C. Yohn. Continental Insurance Company, New York

before—the result of drill and discipline under the Prussian master, General von Steuben. Rallying behind Washington at the Battle of Monmouth, they drove the enemy from the field in what proved to be the last major combat of the war's stalemated northern sector.

The British turned south, counting on Loyalist support. Under Sir Henry Clinton who had replaced General Howe as overall commander, they seized Savannah and Charleston, then invaded the backlands and ran into hornet nests of guerrillas, led by Washington's able Rhode Island general, Nathanael Greene.

"We fight, get beat, rise and fight again," wrote Greene after a series of battles that left the Redcoats jolted even in victory.

In the end, George Washington brought off a feat of military strategy such as every general dreams of. Its goal was Yorktown, Virginia, on a small peninsula between the York and James Rivers, where Britain's Lord Cornwallis had massed his troops.

Washington's grand plan was set by mid-August, 1781. His first move was to lead his main Continental Army on a secret march south from the Hudson River region, in New York. With him went Count Rochambeau's French Expeditionary Force. At the same time, a French fleet under Admiral de

Martha Washington and neighbors greet General Washington and his colleague, the French commander, Count de Rochambeau, on their way south to the crucial Battle of Yorktown. The overnight stop at Mount Vernon, in September 1781, was the first time that Washington had seen his plantation home since the war began.

Painting by John Ward Dunsmore. Courtesy Fraunces Tavern Museum, Sons of the Revolution, New York

In a symbolic ceremony, Washington fires his army's first shot in the Battle of Yorktown. The confrontation, which had begun on September 28, 1781, found the besieged troops of Cornwallis facing a French fleet under Admiral de Grasse in Chesapeake Bay, plus the combined forces of Washington and Rochambeau on the land side. As the pressure of fierce bombardment and bayonet charges mounted, Cornwallis sent out a young drummer with a white flag to seek a parley. Complete surrender came on October 19.

Painting by Clyde O. DeLand. Continental Insurance Company, New York

Washington receives an emissary from Cornwallis asking for a truce during the Battle of Yorktown. The scene depicts Washington's headquarters on October 17, 1781, at which time the American commander granted a cease fire of only 2 hours instead of the 24 hours requested. This life-size fresco decorates the Members' private dining room in the House Wing of the United States Capitol. The artist was Constantino Brumidi, famous for his long, dedicated service in embellishing the Capitol.

Courtesy Architect of the Capitol

Grasse raced north from the West Indies to block Cornwallis's escape by the Chesapeake Bay.

Washington's land-and-sea strategy went as smoothly as those of a master chess player. On reaching Williamsburg, 13 miles from Cornwallis's base, he and Rochambeau joined forces with Lafayette, already a veteran of early Virginia fighting. From Williamsburg the Allied armies marched on to join De Grasse's fleet surrounding Cornwallis's trapped encampment at Yorktown.

The siege began September 28, as 17,000 American and French troops launched a series of attacks on British defenses from the land side. Nineteen days later, Cornwallis—outnumbered two to one and shattered by bombardments—appealed for terms.

Formal surrender came October 19, 1781. Under a warm afternoon sun, the British troops filed out glumly to lay down their arms. As they moved slowly along to the shrill sound of fifes playing old English tunes, they doubtless heard one whose title has enlivened historic accounts ever since. It was called, aptly enough, "The World Turned Upside Down."

The Revolution was won, though British acknowledgment was still nearly two years away. To George and Martha Washington, this dreary, anticlimactic time brought deep personal tragedy. On the heels of the Yorktown triumph, Martha's only son, 27-year-old Jackie Custis, succumbed to "camp fever" contracted while serving as a personal aide to the General.

Following the funeral, the Washingtons took Jackie's widow for a temporary stay at Mount Vernon, where she had left her four children. Later they would rear as their own the two younger ones—Eleanor (or "Nelly"), who was named for her mother, and George Washington Parke Custis.

But there was still an anxious waiting period before final peace. The interval involved a few scattered skirmishes with the Indians on the western frontier, and here and there abroad an engagement between the British and their French and Spanish enemies carrying on the struggle.

After Yorktown, General Washington set up his last headquarters at Newburgh on the Hudson for his remaining troops. Martha was with him, too, for the last time in the eight years of war that she had shared the army's headquarters between campaigns.

Though Washington's men grew restive with the inactivity and delay, the good news finally came. The peace treaty was signed at Paris on September 3, 1783.

There remained only the formality of disbanding the Continental Army at Newburgh, and Washington's triumphant entry into New York and a few other cities. He bade a tender, tearful farewell to his officers at Fraunces Tavern in New York, resigned his commission to Congress (then meeting at Annapolis, Maryland), and reached Mount Vernon just in time to celebrate Christmas Eve, 1783.

"I am now a private Citizen on the banks of the Powtowmack," he wrote a former colleague with quiet satisfaction as he slipped back into the routine of home and farm.

The death of 27-year-old John Parke Custis brings grief to Martha and George Washington at the moment of national triumph over victory at Yorktown. During the battle, "Jackie"—Martha's son and a volunteer aide to his stepfather—became ill of what was called camp fever. He lived to see the ceremony of British defeat, but died soon after. This miniature of John Parke was painted by Charles Willson Peale in 1772.

Courtesy The Mount Vernon Ladies' Association of the Union

This medal, one of a series produced by the United States Capitol Historical Society, depicts the signing of the Treaty of Paris that ended the American Revolution on September 3, 1783. Sculptured by Mico Kaufman, the obverse side represents America's chief Commissioners, Benjamin Franklin, John Jay, and John Adams. The reverse side presents part of the treaty document, surmounted by a map of the Thirteen Original Colonies.

Courtesy U.S. Capitol Historical Society

During the precarious period following the Yorktown victory of October 1781, General Washington set up his last army headquarters at Newburgh, New York. Here he anxiously awaited news of the signing of the peace treaty with the British. And here, in the fall of 1782, Martha joined him for the last time in the eight war years she had shared winter quarters with him and his troops.

Washington, a Biography by Benson J. Lossing

Washington disbands his Continental Army at Newburgh on the Hudson late in October 1783, after learning that the peace treaty ending the Revolution had finally been signed at Paris on September 3, 1783.

Engraving by A. B. Walter. District of Columbia Public Library, Washingtoniana Division

As New Yorkers cheer, Washington makes a triumphant entrance into their city on November 25, 1783. The arrival marks the end of the seven years that the British held this major American port.

Engraving by P. Greatbach after Chapin. *Washington, a Biography* by Benson J. Lossing

In an emotion-packed scene, Washington says farewell to his officers (December 4, 1783) in Fraunces Tavern, New York. While others wait their turn, the Army's Commander-in-Chief embraces Henry Knox, who made victory possible at Dorchester Heights by transporting the necessary cannon from Fort Ticonderoga.

Engraving by Phillibrown of painting by Alonzo Chappel. *Life and Times of Washington* by John Frederick Schroeder

On Christmas Eve, 1783, Mount Vernon welcomes home a rider with destiny who had spent eight years leading his men through joy and sorrow, defeat and triumph.

Photograph by Ted Spiegel

At long last Washington also could revive his projects to develop Dismal Swamp in southern Virginia, and to cut a canal linking Chesapeake Bay with the Ohio River by way of the Potomac. To chart the canal route and inspect his own outlying lands, he again rode the trail westward in 1784.

But the hero of the Revolution could not escape the penalty of fame. He was swamped with correspondence. His home was like "a well resorted tavern," he remarked, "as scarcely any strangers . . . going from north to south, or from south to north, do not spend a day or two at it."

Nor could Washington ignore the chaos threatening the weak and divided nation. "There are combustibles in every State," he wrote, after Shays' Rebellion over hard times had revealed unrest in Massachusetts.

From retirement, Washington argued for a strong central government to replace the loose Confederation under which the states had operated since 1781. "Thirteen Sovereignties pulling against each other, and all tugging at the Federal head," he warned, "will soon bring ruin."

Torn between his desire to leave public life and the need for action, Washington agreed to head the Virginia delegation to the Constitutional Convention, held in May 1787, at Philadelphia. There he was unanimously elected the Convention's president.

Americans owe much to George Washington for their Constitution. Though as presiding officer he took small part in debates that raged through the long, hot summer, universal respect for his integrity and judgment was a vital factor in securing the Constitution's adoption and ratification.

To Washington himself, the forming of a national government from "so many different States" seemed "little short of a miracle," as he wrote Lafayette.

Pennsylvania delegate Benjamin Franklin put it another way. He had often looked toward a painting of the sun behind the presiding officer's chair, he said, and wondered about its direction. "At length," he concluded, "I have the happiness to know it is a rising and not a setting sun."

Greeting his friends and neighbors on Christmas Day, 1783, Washington believed that he was returning for good to his beloved estate by the Potomac. Instead, fate held in store more surprises and achievements for the victorious commander of the Revolution.

Private Collection

CHAPTER 6

The Republic Takes a President

NATURALLY, WASHINGTON WAS FIRST CHOICE as President of the new Republic. Typically, he accepted the office with reluctance, and, aged by burdens at 57, he had modest doubts of being able to fulfill it.

"My movements to the chair of Government," he wrote wryly after learning of his unanimous election, "will be accompanied by feelings not unlike those of a culprit who is going to the place of his execution."

The land-poor President-elect had to borrow money to settle his affairs and pay travel expenses to his own inaugural in the temporary capital of New York. But he was both touched and pleased by the cheering crowds and ardent tributes—including gun salutes, flowers, pageants, and poetry—that met him at almost every stop.

On April 30, 1789, when he took the oath of office on a balcony of New York's Federal Hall, eager spectators jammed the streets and watched from windows and roofs.

A "silent tearful ecstacy . . . pervaded the myriads who witnessed the scene," one recalled 60 years later.

For the tough job ahead, President Washington would need all his popularity, wisdom, and experience. Most helpful was the loving support of Martha who was already winning hearts by her unassuming warmth as the first First Lady of the new Republic.

In August 1790 the Washingtons moved with their roving government to another temporary seat at Philadelphia, where the affairs of state were to be administered until a permanent capital by the Potomac could be built and readied for occupancy in 1800.

These were perilous times for the infant nation that was attempting to organize a country and a capital city on the edge of a vast, unexplored continent. In fact, from his first day in office, Washington faced an assortment of foreign and domestic crises as challenging in his time as any we know today.

For one troubling event, the French Revolution that had erupted in 1789 was sending tremors across the Atlantic. Though Washington, like many other

OPPOSITE:
Standing on the open gallery of New York's old City Hall (later called Federal Hall), Washington takes the oath of office on April 30, 1789. Among the distinguished military and civilian leaders sharing this historic moment is Vice President John Adams, destined to become America's second President eight years afterward.

Drawing by H. A. Ogden, Harper's Weekly, May 11, 1889. Library of Congress

The Constitutional Convention, held at Philadelphia in 1787, established the future form of United States government. As the elected president of the Convention, Washington presided over deliberations by many of the young Republic's leading citizens, including the venerable Benjamin Franklin. The result was the replacement of the loose Articles of Confederation between individual states by a national constitution.

Painting by H. Hintermeister. Courtesy Fraunces Tavern Museum, Sons of the Revolution, New York

With flowers, poetry, and pageants, citizens of the new nation greet Washington on his way to his first presidential inaugural. At each stop between Mount Vernon and New York City, crowds gathered to show their gratitude for his services to their country. This nineteenth-century illustration of the event depicts young Angelica (daughter of the famous artist Charles Willson Peale) as she leans from an overhanging branch to crown Washington with a hero's laurel wreath.

Illustration by F. O. C. Darley. *Our Country* by Benson J. Lossing

Americans, sympathized with fellow revolutionists, he would soon find reason for concern over the violent differences that led to the Reign of Terror. Its arrests and executions, including the guillotining of Louis XVI and his queen, Marie Antoinette, shocked and repelled him.

At home, the adjacent colonial territories held by the French and Spanish, along with the Northwest outposts that the British stubbornly refused to give up, raised problems that were not only political but interwoven with needs of American trade, transportation, and free access to ports. And, as if these conflicting European interests were not enough, there were the hostile Indian tribes on the various frontiers to be dealt with by military means and treaties.

Moreover, in addition to the international affairs that demanded his attention, Washington had the ultimate responsibility of organizing a bold experiment in self rule.

"I walk on untrodden ground," he wrote, after appointing his first Cabinet officers and improvising guidelines for executive cooperation with Congress. Among his responsibilities was also naming the Chief Justice of the United States and other members of the Supreme Court.

To Washington, his initial steps meant laying the foundation for a country whose power and dignity would be rooted in strong central control. Such a

President-elect Washington receives a tumultuous welcome on his arrival in the harbor of the temporary National Capital at New York City. Surrounded by small boats filled with cheering spectators, saluted by bursts of artillery fire on shore, he acknowledges the honors paid him from his flag-decorated barge.

Engraving by J. Rogers after J. McNevin

Thomas Jefferson and Alexander Hamilton—Secretaries of State and Treasury respectively (from left)—confer with President Washington as members of his first Cabinet. In philosophical beliefs and practical application, the two men stood at opposite poles. Perhaps only Washington could have resolved the conflicts that developed, and thus obtained the diplomatic and financial results required. This mural by the dedicated Italian artist, Constantino Brumidi, can be seen today in the Senate Reception Room of the United States Capitol at Washington, D.C.

Courtesy Architect of the Capitol

philosophy naturally put him on the side of the emerging Federalists, who opposed the "liberals" of the states' rights faction. The liberals, notably Thomas Jefferson, made up the early Republican Party that would later rename itself the Democratic Party.

But Washington's innate fairness and his faith in his country's institutions would not permit him to practice favoritism. Hence, in his first appointments of men to head the executive departments established by Congress, he selected Federalist Alexander Hamilton to be the conservative Secretary of the Treasury, and Republican Jefferson to be Secretary of State.

As it turned out, the contributions of these men played major, though radically different, roles in helping Washington to achieve remarkable progress and political balance in his national objectives.

Hamilton's Treasury programs—including Federal assumption of the states' Revolutionary debts, the creation of a national bank, and measures to aid manufacturing and trade—gave the United States firm credit standing in the world.

Jefferson, as Secretary of State from 1790 to 1793, when the office involved "home" as well as foreign affairs, brought to the first American administration a lasting sense of the rights and humanity of the common man.

On the international front, Washington signed a controversial treaty with England in 1795, and another with Spain that was rated a diplomatic triumph. The Spanish treaty resolved the President's frontier problems over Florida's boundaries, and opened American navigation of the Mississippi, along with port facilities at New Orleans.

Successful military campaigns against the Indians quieted much of that turmoil, and led to British evacuation of their northwest forts. And, perhaps most important of all, the nation managed to maintain neutrality during the hazardous seagoing war that raged for years between France and England.

That Washington accomplished these vital goals in spite of conflicting opinions and personalities has long brought expressions of wonder and admiration from scholars and historians. Certainly, his calm judgment and patience in mediating the frequent and often bitter disputes between his two strong-minded Cabinet members, Jefferson and Hamilton, were essential factors in the successful outcome of seemingly intractable difficulties.

During his second term, the President himself endured partisan criticism and abuse from the press and the public over his administrative acts and the formal social etiquette he adopted to lend prestige to his office. ". . . until within the last year or two ago, I had no conception that Parties would, or even could go, the length I have been witness to," Washington wrote Jefferson in July 1796, ". . . nor did I believe . . . that every act of my administration would be tortured, and the grossest, and most insidious mis-representations of them be made . . . in such exaggerated and indecent terms as could scarcely be applied to a Nero; a notorious defaulter, or even to a common pickpocket."

The first United States Supreme Court met in this New York building at the foot of Broad Street in February 1790. Appointed by President Washington in accordance with the Constitution, its six members were Chief Justice John Jay (above) and five Associate Justices. The number of Justices has varied through the years, but has remained at nine since 1869.

F. O. C. Darley. *Our Country* by Benson J. Lossing

Emmet Collection, New York Public Library *(left)*

President Washington escorts his Indian guests on a walk along Broadway in New York City. When the Republic was young and Indian problems played a crucial role in land policy, Washington invited this Creek chief and his tribal advisers to visit New York and discuss a treaty of friendship. The chief, whose unlikely name—Alexander McGillivray—came from a Scottish-trader father, accepted the invitation, and in August 1790 signed the desired treaty.

Illustration by A. J. Keller. *Harper's Monthly Magazine*, October 1899

As the nation's first "First Lady," Martha Washington holds a reception, or levee, in a style romanticized by this nineteenth-century print. Though the Washingtons' personal tastes were simple, they entertained officially with stately elegance to show the world that the head of their new country was due as much respect as that accorded European monarchs. Such lavishness brought criticism of the President on occasion, not only from political enemies but in milder form, from friends.

District of Columbia Public Library, Washingtoniana Division

Alighting from his state coach-and-six at Philadelphia's Independence Hall, President Washington prepares to take his second oath of office in the nation's final temporary capital. The date is March 4, 1793. Behind him lies his first term and the establishment of a brand-new form of government. Ahead stretch four more years of bold experiment in self rule during a dangerous period of international and domestic turmoil.

Painting by J. L. G. Ferris, Archives of '76, Bay Village, Ohio

After declining a third-term bid in 1796, Washington hosts his last official dinner as President. Among his distinguished guests was President-elect John Adams, who would serve four years from March 4, 1797. Outgoing President Washington set a precedent before his departure by attending the inaugural ceremony of his successor in the Philadelphia Senate Chamber.

Illustration by A. J. Keller. *Harper's Monthly Magazine*, November 1899

On returning to these pleasant Mount Vernon surroundings at the end of his Presidency, Washington was at last home to stay. From the time he first left to fight in the French and Indian War of the 1750's, he had looked forward to fulfilling his lifelong dream of improving and developing his estate. Yet again and again he was called away to serve his country: To lead the Revolution for eight long years; then another eight to lead the young Republic on an uncharted course. The last short span of Washington's life was a happy one, however, spent in cultivating his fields and enjoying his friends and family.

Engraving by J. Duthie after G. I. Parkyns. Mount Vernon by Benson J. Lossing. Courtesy The Society of the Cincinnati

Thus, after 45 years in his country's service through good and bad times, President Washington felt free to decline a third-term effort in 1796.

As "a parting friend," he published his Farewell Address, urging his countrymen to cherish their liberty and union, to shun "the fury" of party politics and foreign entanglements.

Then, once more as in that honeymoon spring long before, Mr. and Mrs. Washington—accompanied by granddaughter Nelly Custis, three coaches of household goods, plus a parrot and a dog—took the road home to Mount Vernon.

"No consideration under heaven that I can foresee," Washington vowed, "shall again withdraw me from the walks of private life."

But the unexpected happened. In 1798, undeclared war broke out between France and the United States over American shipping rights. President John Adams appointed Washington to head the army; Washington's stern sense of duty would not let him refuse.

The struggle was fought at sea. The General was never called to field duty, though he traveled to Philadelphia for conferences, and military correspondence added heavily to his usual activities at Mount Vernon.

Soon, however, following a successful peace negotiated by President Adams, Farmer Washington was back in the smooth furrow of the life he loved. He was content now, he said, "to make, and sell a little flour . . . to repair houses . . . and to amuse myself in Agricultural and rural pursuits."

A happy interruption to his daily round was the marriage, on Washington's 67th birthday in February 1799, of charming Nelly Custis to his favorite nephew, Lawrence Lewis.

The couple stayed on at Mount Vernon, waiting for their own home, Woodlawn, to be built on 2,000 acres of adjoining land provided them by the General. Their first child was born at Mount Vernon late in November.

But time was running out for Great-uncle George. After riding about his farms through driving snow and sleet on December 12, he wrote in his diary of a "large circle round the Moon last night," and noted continuing snow and hail, turning "to a settled cold Rain."

The next day he complained of sore throat and chills. His condition worsened and was followed by complications that defied three attending physicians and at least three bloodlettings.

Before midnight, December 14, 1799, George Washington was dead—peacefully and at home, his Martha near him.

It was the end of a century, and of an era for a country about to embark on an unknown future.

It was also the end of the 10-year period set aside by Congress for the creation of its future capital amid the rolling hills, woodlands, and marshes that framed the broad Potomac.

In less than six months of Washington's death, President John Adams and his Cabinet chiefs began preparing for "the prudent and economical" removal of the public offices from Philadelphia.

Together with the 131 clerks and aides who would make up the Federal City's first bureaucracy they traveled by carriage, horseback, and stagecoach, while shipping most of the government's papers and furniture by sloop.

Just how their village capital had come into being is a story that forms an integral part of George Washington's own biography. For no other public service came closer to his heart, and to it he devoted much of his time and energy during the last decade of his life.

In the day-by-day difficulties he met along the way lies a tale of cliff-hanging suspense, dismaying delays, and joy-filled accomplishments.

We can read of these events now in the correspondence, diaries, and documents left behind by Washington and his colleagues. They give us a new sense of the human dimension and the personal adventures involved in the founding of the city called Washington, District of Columbia.

Surrounding George Washington's casket before the old family tomb at Mount Vernon, stand high-ranking Masons and Episcopal clergy taking part in the formal ceremonies, along with army officers, honor guard, friends and relatives from the neighborhood. Many others, including close kin of the Washingtons' were prevented from attending because of the suddenness of the tragedy. Mrs. Washington herself remained in the mansion with her granddaughter Nelly Custis for solace. Within less than three years, Martha Washington's body was placed here beside that of her husband. And in 1831 the remains of both were removed to the newly built tomb nearby.

District of Columbia Public Library. Washingtoniana Division

PART TWO

A CAPITAL IS BORN

The permanent capital of the United States had its beginning in an incident outside this New York building. In it President Washington lived during part of the 1789 period when the city was temporary seat of government. Here on Broadway, Secretary of Treasury Hamilton met Secretary of State Jefferson, and persuaded him to support a compromise by which the Federal City would be located in the rural Potomac Valley in exchange for national assumption of state debts from the Revolution.

Harper's Monthly Magazine, October 1899

On this sketch map of the Thirteen Original States, the city named for George Washington stands midway between north and south—the location chosen by Congress in 1790 for the Republic's future capital. Shown here also are the leading cities of the time, including New York and Philadelphia— in turn capitals of the Constitutional United States. Both waged vigorous campaigns to retain their status. Philadelphia's political machinations particularly worried President Washington, who once remarked that the enemies of the Potomac site would "leave no means unessayed to injure it." Washington's own estate at Mount Vernon lay 15 miles downriver.

Map by Geraldine Linder

CHAPTER 1

Politics Clears the Way

$\mathcal{E}$VERY CITY HAS ITS OWN PERSONALITY, a distillation drawn from location, history, and the impact of the men and women who, from the beginning, have left their mark on it.

Among the great capitals of the world, Washington, District of Columbia, is unique in striking ways. For one thing, its history is so short. Only a scant two centuries have passed since geographic location—and partisan politics—made it the seat of government for a brash new nation that stretched then in a fragile chain of thirteen states along the eastern seaboard.

For another formative influence going back to its establishment by Congress in 1790, the Federal City was intimately associated with those remarkable contemporaries we call the Founding Fathers. All of them—John Adams, Thomas Jefferson, and James Madison among others—had fought in one way or another to win independence from England's George III. With that goal accomplished, they went on to serve as Presidents, Members of Congress, and diplomats sent abroad to represent the fledgling Republic as it sought to plant its roots in a continent whose extent and wealth were still undreamed of.

Standing tall among these men, of course, was George Washington, whose birth in February 1732 provided a fine, round-number anniversary of 250 years in 1982.

As the victorious commander of the Revolution and the first elected President of the United States, Washington found himself at the center of events that would bring about the choice of the permanent capital site beside the banks of the Potomac River.

That all-important decision was made in New York City, where the nation's first temporary capital had been set up under the Constitution in 1789, with George Washington at its head.

It was also a decision born of bitter political controversy and questionable compromise, though you would never have guessed it from the casual, matter-of-fact statements recorded in President Washington's diary for July 12, 1790.

"Exercised on Horseback between 5 and 6 in the morning," he wrote.

PRECEDING SPREAD:
Looking across the Potomac toward the Maryland shore, this charming view from Mount Vernon has been preserved in a painting made by architect-artist Benjamin Henry Latrobe. On a visit to Washington's home in 1796, as he noted in his journal, Latrobe found the President most hospitable and good-humored. Mrs. Washington, he wrote, "retains strong remains of considerable beauty," and he was enchanted by her granddaughter, Nelly Custis, whom he described as having "more perfection of form . . . and of firmness of mind than I have ever seen before or conceived consistent with mortality."

Maryland Historical Society

"... And about Noon had ... presented to me by the joint Committee of Congress ... An Act for Establishing the Temporary and permanent Seat of the Government of the United States."

This historic legislation, which the President signed into law on July 16, provided that the nation's future capital would be built in open country along the shores of the Potomac, and that Philadelphia would become the temporary seat of government during a ten-year interlude of construction.

The solution settled the long-disputed problem of the Republic's permanent capital, but it did not prevent advocates of New York, Philadelphia, and Baltimore, among other towns and cities that had competed for the honor—and economic advantages—from continuing to carry on a kind of propaganda war against the Potomac project itself. Nor did it silence criticism of the compromise that had been reached between political leaders, and which involved widespread speculation and huge financial scandals.

The story of that curious incident in American politics had begun earlier in the year of 1790, when Alexander Hamilton, as the Secretary of the Treasury, lobbied unsuccessfully to persuade Congress to vote federal responsibility for state debts incurred during the Revolution.

Members of Congress from the northern states, which had more to gain from larger and still unpaid debts, chiefly favored "Assumption." Those from the South, where the debts were smaller and the people less able to pay the federal taxes required, strongly opposed the action. Big mercantile, shipping, and real estate operators promoted their own interests, and the differences between the conflicting groups threatened to tear the shaky nation apart.

In Hamilton's fertile mind, a possible deal took form. In exchange for federal takeover of state debts, he proposed that the Nation's Capital be situated closer to the South, as desired by then House Representative James Madison of Virginia, and other prominent southerners.

In promoting his idea among potential supporters, Hamilton found an unlikely ally in Thomas Jefferson when he encountered the Secretary of State, either by accident or design, in front of President Washington's New York residence on Broadway.

As Jefferson recalled the meeting later, "Hamilton was in despair . . . He walked me backwards and forwards before the President's door for half an hour. He painted pathetically ... the danger of the secession ... and the separation of the States. He observed ... that a common duty should make it a common concern ... and that the question having been lost by a small majority only, it was probable that an appeal from me to ... some of my friends might affect a change in the vote."

Jefferson replied that he would do what he could to avert "a dissolution of our Union at this incipient stage." He therefore invited Hamilton to dine with him shortly, together with "another friend or two ... to form a compromise which was to save the Union."

The bargain was struck at Jefferson's dinner, conducted with his usual

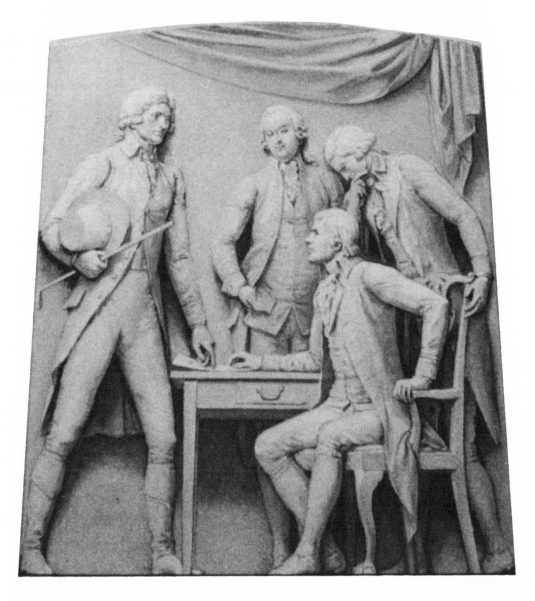

The first Federal Commissioners of the District of Columbia meet with Washington's chief consultant Jefferson on details concerning the planning and building of the future capital. In 1790, Congress had authorized President Washington to choose the exact area along the Potomac River where the new city would rise. It also directed him to appoint three Commissioners to help carry out the objective. These men— Thomas Johnson, Daniel Carroll, and David Stuart—were all leading citizens of the region, as well as personal friends and longtime colleagues of Washington's.

Courtesy Architect of the Capitol

charm and hospitality—though he observed that one of the Virginians present had agreed to it "with a revulsion of stomach almost convulsive."

The result was the passage on July 16, 1790, of the so-called Residency Bill" directing that the permanent capital be established beside the Potomac. By August 2, Congress had enacted Hamilton's debt-funding proposal, which Washington signed on August 4.

There was plenty of grumbling over the deal, and dismay that so many speculators would be enriched at the expense of those who would be swindled out of their legal rights. Critics also made fun of "that Indian place" picked from the wilds. One newspaper reporter, in the classical rhetoric of the day, quipped that "Potomacus" was the offspring of the seduction of "Miss Assumption" by "Mr. Residence."

But the choice was made, and the Potomac area had real advantages. It was located midway between northern and southern states, and its natural setting, framed by river and wooded hills, was superb. Along the winding shore of its river stretch lay two already flourishing ports—Alexandria, Virginia, and Georgetown, Maryland. In the west, the Potomac Valley offered land and water routes for potential transportation deep into the continental interior.

Even more important to the ultimate success of the undertaking was another factor, seldom remembered today. With full confidence in the good sense and enormous prestige of their President, the lawmakers authorized Washington to select the exact site of the future capital, and to have the final say in all practical details of building a city in what was then a region of farms and forests.

To assist him in this assignment, Congress instructed Washington to appoint three Federal Commissioners to work under his direction in carrying out the project. It also designated a specific territory within which he was to decide on the boundaries of the Federal City. This territory, as the legislators stated in the same Residency Bill, should cover an area "not exceeding 10 miles square," and be situated specifically "at some place" between the mouths of the Eastern Branch, now the Anacostia River, and the Conococheague, an Indian-named tributary entering the Potomac some 80 miles upstream. The only other limitation on Washington's judgment (covered in a later amendment) was that all public buildings must be built on the Maryland side.

Finally, as a crowning commitment, the President and his Commissioners were charged with providing "suitable" buildings for the accommodation of Congress and the President, and for the public officers of the Government of the United States.

It was a staggering enterprise. No other government, with the exception of Tsarist Russia under the iron rule of Peter the Great, had ever created a brand-new capital.

Furthermore, Congress appropriated no funds to build its Federal City. Instead, "for defraying the expense of . . . purchases and buildings, the President of the United States was authorized and requested to accept grants of money."

The new Treasury had, indeed, no money in 1790 for so large and costly a venture. Virginia and Maryland, which had ceded to the Federal Government their jurisdiction over land to be used for the capital, also agreed to furnish $120,000 and $72,000, respectively, toward construction of public buildings. But these funds were still merely in the promised stage.

Thus Washington was forced to seek the necessary credit and cash from the only source then available—the land itself. This meant that he would have to negotiate with individual owners to obtain legal title to their properties, and somehow find the cash to pay for land that would be required for public use, as well as for the running expenses of designing and constructing the Federal buildings.

No one seemed to doubt President Washington's ability to accomplish these formidable tasks. And from the alacrity with which he went about the job, it appeared that he, too, felt that his assignment was both reasonable and achievable.

CHAPTER 2

Washington Launches His Project

LESS THAN TWO MONTHS AFTER SIGNING the Residency Bill, President Washington made his first official trip to the capital site by the Potomac. During the intervening period, he had found time to visit Rhode Island, which only recently had become the thirteenth state to ratify the Constitution. And he had moved with his administration to the nation's last temporary capital at Philadelphia.

As he began his long and arduous adventure of city building, Washington could count on at least one practical advantage. His own plantation home at Mount Vernon, only 15 miles from Georgetown, offered a convenient base of operation.

He arrived there from Philadelphia on September 11, 1790, during the lull of the Congressional recess, and proceeded to organize his preliminary plans. Jefferson and Madison soon followed for discussions on the project, for both were keenly interested in its success, and both were prepared to further it by using their influence with landowners of the area. Jefferson, particularly, would play a major role in advising the President on many of the city-planning problems that arose—though Washington did not always follow his consultant's suggestions.

But first it was Washington's sole responsibility to establish the capital city's boundaries within the area outlined by Congress. Thus, on October 15, he left Mount Vernon for Georgetown, to begin his tour of exploration and decision.

From Georgetown, on the morning of the 16th, he set out—as reported in the local *Times and Patowmack Packet*—to inspect the vicinity "with the principal citizens of this town and neighborhood . . . in order to fix on a proper selection for the Grand Columbian Federal City."

Some of his companions on that day-long ride through the countryside were doubtless among the landowners who had just handed him a written offer to sell their holdings on any terms he felt reasonable. With their proposal went a glowing description of the advantages that would result from acquiring their properties in a region that would "at once contribute to the beauty, health and security of a city intended for the seat of empire."

It was too early for commitments, however. The following morning, Washington was again on the move. This time he followed the Potomac route all the way to the northern limits of the river's shore set by Congress at Conococheague Creek.

Wherever he went, he was greeted by volunteers eager to lend their assistance in bringing the prestigious capital site—and anticipated real-estate profits —to their doorstep. As Washington and his party approached Elizabeth-Town (now Hagerstown), they were met by the community's leading citizens with a troop of light horse. Closer in, they were joined by an escort of militia, and welcomed to the city with the ringing of bells and the "applause of the gratified inhabitants [for] the illustrious stranger," as the town paper, the *Washington Spy*, called the President. That evening, the account went on, the "town was illuminated, bonfires appeared in all quarters and every demonstration of joy was exhibited on the happy occasion."

The happy occasion included a supper at Mr. Beltzhoover's Tavern, followed by the customary numerous toasts. Washington himself proposed one: "To the River Patowmac. May the residence law be perpetuated and Patowmac view the Federal City."

Up early on October 21, Washington received a delegation of Elizabeth-Town citizens, who were not above sweetening their approval of this sentiment by a bit of flattery. They would be honored, said their spokesman, "to be included within your more especial command and jurisdiction . . . the grand centre of virtues."

In his response, the President was courteous, as always, but the people of Elizabeth-Town gained no more from their flattery than the landowners had won with their offer to sell at any price.

Washington's last stop on the trip brought him to Williamsport, a few miles southwest of Hagerstown. From this point, where the Conococheague empties into the Potomac, he took passage, in the words of an ardent admirer writing in the *Washington Spy*, "down that noble river (the American Thames) which will be proud to waft him home."

Wafted back to Mount Vernon, Washington stayed on there for another month before returning to Philadelphia for the reconvening of Congress. It was hardly a restful interlude, with the appeals of various bidders for a place in the national sun still ringing in his ears, and new ones constantly being echoed.

Soon after his visit to Williamsport, county residents had petitioned the Maryland Assembly to pass an act appropriating a ten-mile-square district should it please the President to place the permanent capital within their jurisdiction. If that hoped-for choice occurred, they said, they were "willing to make every contribution toward the necessary accommodation of Congress that can reasonably be expected or that our circumstances can afford. . . ."

A little later, a news story from Shepherdstown, Virginia (south of Williamsport on the other side of the river) announced that people there were collecting subscriptions to pay for potential Federal buildings. But any money so obtained, the story's author added cautiously, could be used only if "the seat of the federal government will be fixed opposite to this town on the Maryland shore and one-half of the ten mile square will be located in Virginia."

Despite the clamor and pressures, Washington managed to keep the public from learning of his decision until January 24, 1791.

On that day he issued a proclamation from Philadelphia ending all rival hopes. In it, as he also advised Congress in an accompanying message, he announced his selection of "a part of the territory of ten miles square on both sides of the river Potomac so as to comprehend Georgetown in Maryland and to extend to the Eastern Branch...."

This country road, rolling down to the Potomac River through Georgetown, resembles many of the rural areas that Washington visited in 1790 on his upriver travels to seek a suitable location for the Federal Capital. After the trip, he announced that his decision was "to comprehend Georgetown in Maryland and to extend to the Eastern Branch [the Anacostia River]," as part of the 10-mile-square territory designated by Congress.

Engraving by George Isham Parkyns. New York Public Library

The thriving tobacco port of Georgetown, whose waterfront is shown here, played a key role in building the city of Washington, D.C. As the nearest settlement to the open Potomac Valley site, Georgetown offered living accommodations for short and long stays by various leaders in the project. President Washington frequently stopped here on trips back and forth between Mount Vernon and Philadelphia, to consult his aides and to see how construction was progressing.

Library of Congress

There was one hitch, however. Washington felt that the Federal District might well be expanded at its lower limits by adding both sides of the Eastern Branch in Maryland, and the town of Alexandria across the river in Virginia.

To that end he suggested that Congress so amend the Residency Bill. And it was a measure of his immense popularity that the lawmakers shortly enacted his proposal without debate.

Looking back today on this give-and-take of shifting territories, we are reminded that in 1846 Virginia reclaimed Alexandria and its entire Virginia shore, leaving the Nation's Capital a lopsided square containing about two-thirds of the original area dictated by the Residency Bill. But that's another story.

In January 1791, about the same time President Washington announced his decision on the capital's permanent site, he fulfilled another Congressional directive by appointing the three Federal Commissioners who would work with him on the nitty-gritty job of building the city.

These men were all his friends and colleagues, as well as pillars of Tidewater society. No less important, they were able professionals who could assist him with legal and executive details. They also owned large properties in the area, which would give them added incentive to promote the undertaking. Whether anybody objected then to what we might now call "conflict of interest" was not brought up. Their integrity and standing were beyond question.

Thomas Johnson of Frederick, Maryland, had supported Colonial rights from the early days of struggle against George III. As a member of the Continental Congress of 1775, he nominated Washington to be commander-in-chief of the Army. From 1777 to 1779, he had served as Maryland's first governor.

Johnson was Chief Judge of Maryland when Washington named him to the Board of Commissioners for the Federal District. In 1791, the President also appointed him Associate Justice to the United States Supreme Court, a position he continued to hold while acting as a District Commissioner.

But the longest and closest association between the two men was their abiding interest in the "Potowmack Company"—predecessor of the also ill-fated Chesapeake and Ohio Canal. Through this enterprise, Washington dreamed of creating a link with the west by building a series of waterways around the Potomac falls from Chesapeake Bay to the Ohio River. Their project failed because of inherent problems of terrain, but eventually the canal venture would lose out to the competition of America's young and booming railroad industry.

The second Commissioner was Daniel Carroll, also of Maryland, who was known as Carroll of Rock Creek to distinguish him from his namesake nephew of Duddington. A leading citizen of wealth and influence, the elder Carroll had been a delegate to the Continental Congress that ratified the Articles of Confederation, then served at the Constitutional Convention of 1787. Two years later, he was elected Maryland Representative to the First Congress of the United States. He finished his term just in time to take on the duties of Washington's Federal Commission.

David Stuart, third member of the Board of Commissioners, was a Virginian. As one of Washington's family physicians and the husband of Eleanor Custis—widow of Martha's son John Parke Custis—Stuart was undoubtedly the most intimate of the Commissioners in relation to the President. From existing details in diaries and other sources, and from the extensive correspondence carried on between the two men on national and personal matters, it is evident that Washington had a high regard for the doctor's advice and opinion, and that he found added comfort in the family connection.

So both the players and the script appeared promising as the curtain rose on the first act of the making of the new capital. In this drama there would be many leading men. Soon the original cast would include an authentic but temperamental genius destined to leave his mark on the city for all time.

CHAPTER 3

The President and the City Planner

His name was Pierre Charles L'Enfant. Born at Paris in 1754, he was the son of a Court artist, the landscape painter Pierre L'Enfant, examples of whose work are still exhibited at Versailles.

Young Pierre Charles studied at the Royal Academy of Painting and Sculpture in Paris. He showed special talent in the fine art of landscape painting, which in his militaristic society included fortifications. He was familiar, too, with the advances made by the great French architects and landscape designers, then considered to be practicing a branch of engineering. He could not have failed to know of their influence on the development of city planning.

All of these factors were part of the young man's background and would play a large part in his future. But Pierre Charles was also a rebel and an idealist. He volunteered to fight for the American Revolution in 1776, and in the spring of 1777 he landed in this country, eager for action.

L'Enfant served under General Washington at Valley Forge. He was wounded in action at Savannah, Georgia, and taken prisoner by the British on the American defeat at Charleston, South Carolina. He ended active service with the rank of Brevet Major of Engineers, awarded by special resolution of Congress.

After the war, Major L'Enfant settled in New York, where his skill in architecture won various commissions, as well as the President's admiration. Several assignments came from his own Society of the Cincinnati, the prestigious organization founded by Washington's disbanding officers. In another important commission, he converted New York's old City Hall to the handsome building on whose balcony Washington would be inaugurated.

L'Enfant, however, nurtured a larger and fiercer ambition. Even before Congress decided on the Potomac location for the capital, he wrote to President Washington as his friend and former commanding officer, expressing the hope that he might be allowed to take part in planning the city. ". . . it will be obvious," he said, "that the plan should be drawn on such a scale as to leave

OPPOSITE:
At the Capitol site atop Jenkins Hill, Washington gives final approval, in June 1791, to L'Enfant's location for the home of Congress. "I could discover no one [situation]," the architect had reported to the President, "so advantageously to greet the congressional building as is that on the west end of Jenkins heights . . . It stands as a pedestal," he added, "waiting for a monument."

Mural by Allyn Cox. Courtesy Architect of the Capitol

As an original member of the Society of the Cincinnati, artist-architect L'Enfant designed this insignia for the fraternal order that was founded by Washington's officers at the end of the Revolution. Named for the early Roman general Cincinnatus, the Society was established in each of the Thirteen Original States, with a branch added in France for French officers who had joined in the American struggle for independence. The chief feature of L'Enfant's emblem was the American bald eagle, bearing symbolic medallions on its breast and back. A lavishly jeweled Eagle was presented to General Washington by the French Navy following his election as the Order's first president-general. The present Society includes more than 3,000 members, who share the honor through inheritance.

Courtesy The Society of the Cincinnati

room for that aggrandisement & embellishment which the increase in the wealth of the Nation will permit . . . at any period however remote."

Fortunately for the French dreamer, his vision of the future capital was closer to Washington's idea than was Jefferson's proposal, submitted in the form of a sketch that allowed only 1,500 acres for the seat of what he conceived would be a small, agricultural nation. Washington's decision was to mark off a district four times as big. "If Philadelphia stood upon an area of three by two miles," he commented, "and if the metropolis of one state occupied so much ground, what ought that of the United States to occupy?"

Thus, with their common faith in the future of the Republic, and with L'Enfant's reputation as a brilliant architect, it was not surprising that Washington accepted his application for a share in the Federal City undertaking.

It was hardly an invitation—at least not at once—to lay out the whole city, though L'Enfant, with the confidence of genius, would take it as such.

His first instructions came in a February 1791 letter from Jefferson, acting as the President's executive officer. In this letter, L'Enfant was directed merely to study the contours of the land. At the same time, he was told to give special attention to his "drawing of the particular grounds most likely to be approved for the site of the Federal town and buildings."

In more specific terms, Jefferson instructed L'Enfant to "be pleased to begin on the Eastern branch and proceed from thence upwards, laying down the hills, valleys, morasses and waters between that and the Potomac, the Tyber, and the road leading from Georgetown. . . ."

What L'Enfant did not know as he followed orders was that Washington wanted him to start his survey at the Eastern Branch in order to discourage land speculation elsewhere. If property owners nearer Georgetown saw surveying underway at the far eastern end of the District, Washington remarked, they might "let themselves down to reasonable terms" in disposing of their holdings for public use.

At first all went according to plan. On March 9, 1791, Major L'Enfant rode into Georgetown from the interim capital of Philadelphia. After paying his respects to the port's mayor, he set up headquarters there, and plunged into the work he hoped would mark the crowning achievement of his career.

From the beginning, L'Enfant found his task no sinecure, with bad weather his implacable, all-pervasive enemy; ". . . heavy rain and thick mist which has been incessant ever since my arrival here, does put an insuperable obstacle to my wish of proceeding immediately to the survey," he reported to Jefferson two days after he reached Georgetown. "Should the weather continue bad, as there is every appearance it will, I shall be much at a loss how to make a plan of the ground . . . and have it ready for the President at the time he is expected at this place."

On the other hand, L'Enfant was delighted with the charm and general suitability of the Potomac site. "As far as I was able to judge through a thick fog, I passed on many spots which appeared to me really beautiful," he wrote.

L'Enfant was particularly impressed by one area that would eventually become part of today's downtown city. "The level and extensive ground . . . to the bank of the Potomac as far as Goose [or Tiber] Creek . . ." he observed in the same report to Jefferson, "present a situation most advantageous to run streets and prolong them on grand and far-distant points of view."

L'Enfant was not alone, however, in the rain-drenched marshlands and woods along the Potomac. While he was making his topographic sketches of the region, another Presidential appointee named Andrew Ellicott had been busy since early February running boundary lines for Washington's announced Federal District.

Ellicott was a widely experienced and respected surveyor whose home was then in Philadelphia. On his way to the job, he had hired an assistant— Benjamin Banneker, a talented free black, who had trained himself so well in mathematics and astronomy that he was considered the best man available in the Maryland neighborhood convenient to the capital site.

At this time, President Washington's preliminary program included still another strategem to outwit the speculators he would have to deal with during the coming land negotiations. In letters to several close friends in Georgetown, he enlisted their cooperation to buy up certain properties in strategic locations where the main Federal buildings were likely to rise. As his agents in behalf of the public, these men were asked to observe "the most profound secrecy," and to make their offers as if for themselves.

With all these maneuvers under way, Washington was now ready to depart for Georgetown, where he would confer with the Commissioners, check the work of L'Enfant and Ellicott, and coordinate the other phases of his program.

It is hard for us to realize today just how inconvenient and hazardous travel could be at that time, even for the Chief Executive on official business for his country.

Washington left Philadelphia on March 21, 1791. Since the trip to George-town was only the first leg on a more extensive one he planned through the southern states, he was accompanied by a large and unwieldly entourage. It consisted, he wrote in his diary, "of a Charriot and four horses drove in hand—a light baggage Waggon and two horses—four saddle horses besides a led one for myself—and five—to wit;—my Valet de Chambre, two footmen, Coachmen and postilion."

"Never had Washington faced a more inauspicious start," according to the account in Volume Six of Douglas Southall Freeman's outstanding biography of the first President. "Roads were so heavy with rain and so cut up by wheels that . . . he went down the Eastern Shore of Maryland and undertook to cross the Chesapeake by boat. . . . Everything went wrong. A wagon animal went lame; Washington's saddle horse refused to eat; . . . half a day was lost in

Suter's Tavern, also called Fountain Inn, was one of Georgetown's most popular hostels in Washington's day. Many historic events in the establishment of the National Capital occurred here. Yet the exact location of the tavern was long debated. Then, in the 1950's, Cornelius Heine, a young historian of the National Park Service, undertook a research program through family reminiscenses, tax records, and other sources. The result proved conclusively that Suter's inn had once stood at 31st and K Streets, N.W. This Library of Congress photograph, made around the turn of the twentieth century, together with related research, indicates that the building shown was indeed the same one that had belonged to "Old Suter."

Library of Congress

OPPOSITE:

In this composite painting, produced by Garnet W. Jex as part of his thesis toward a M.F.A. degree from George Washington University, the artist presents eight characters who held leading parts in planning, surveying, and building the capital city. President Washington sits astride his horse at center right. Beside him stands engineer-architect Pierre Charles L'Enfant, displaying his plan of the city. At far right Andrew Ellicott holds his professional instruments, while his assistant, Benjamin Banneker, takes notes. Seen in far-left background are Commissioners Stuart, Johnson, and Carroll, and, just beyond, Dr. William Thornton, designer of the Capitol building.

Courtesy George Washington University

loading . . . a gale sprang up during the sail . . . the little vessel on which Washington had taken passage ran aground twice, and the second time . . . could not be budged. . . ."

In Washington's own graphic description of the night he spent aboard the mired vessel, it was "immensely dark with heavy and variable squals of wind, constant lightning and tremendous thunder. . . . Having lain all night in my Great Coat and boots, in a birth not long enough for me by the head . . . we found ourselves in the morning within about one mile of Anapolis, and still fast aground. . . ."

The Presidential party was rescued by a sailing ship, and Washington himself was landed safely nearby, but the mishaps persisted. As he wrote in his diary, he had "requested Mr. Man [Colonel William Mann] at whose Inn I intended lodging, to send off a Boat to take off two of my Horses and Chariot which I had left on board and with it my coachman to see that it was properly done; but by mistake the latter not having notice of this order and attempting to get on board afterwards in a small sailing boat was overset and narrowly escaped drowning. . . ."

From then on, however, the President's travels were less arduous. After a series of ceremonial escorts, artillery salutes, and formal entertaining by the Governor of Maryland and other distinguished citizens of Annapolis and elsewhere, he finally arrived at Georgetown early on the morning of March 28.

There, while lodging at Suter's Tavern, Washington spent three busy and productive days on the pressing affairs of the Federal City. His first act on arrival was to breakfast with the three Commissioners—Johnson, Carroll, and Stuart.

What they talked about is not recorded, but they must have discussed the evident rivalry among landowners and speculators—each wanting the future public buildings to be located near their own properties.

On that same day, Washington also examined and approved the surveys made so far by Ellicott and L'Enfant, bringing to this scrutiny a practiced eye from his own experiences as a young surveyor in Virginia many years before.

Later, he attended "a public dinner" given at Suter's Tavern by the Mayor and the Corporation of Georgetown, and arranged for another crowded day to come.

The following morning, despite a thick obscuring mist, the President and his Commissioners took an early horseback ride over some of the nearby area marked off by the surveyors. But he "derived no great satisfaction from the review," he said, because of "the unfavorableness of the day."

The historic Forrest (or Marbury) House, which still faces M Street in Georgetown, presents a drab rear view above the old Chesapeake and Ohio Canal. As the once-handsome home of rich landowner Uriah Forrest, this mansion was the scene of a lavish dinner he gave on March 29, 1791, for President Washington and other area property owners. The party was planned at a crucial point in negotiations concerning the proposed Federal City, and it was said that the friendly relations promoted by the festivities enabled Washington to reach favorable terms with the proprietors on transferring their lands to the public.

Watercolor by Earl Minderman, Bethesda, Maryland. Courtesy of the artist

As it turned out, the most useful event of Washington's three-day visit was a conference with the competing landowners which he held at his lodgings that evening.

Writing in his diary later, he recalled that he had warned them "that while each party was aiming to obtain the public buildings, they might, by placing the matter on a contracted scale, defeat the measure altogether...." He also told them that instead of fighting over financial advantage, "they had better, by combining more offers, make a common cause of it."

As a result of this sensible counsel, the President had the satisfaction of learning the next day that the landowners, as he put it, "saw the propriety of my observations. [They] therefore," he continued, "mutually agreed and entered into articles to surrender for public purposes, one half of the land they severally possessed...."

Under the provisions of this March 30 document, the proprietors first promised to convey to President Washington, in trust for the public, all of their holdings within the Federal District. This over-all conveyance was a legal stipulation needed to permit Washington, or any assignees he might appoint, to exercise federal control over the design and development of the future District.

The landowners then followed up their initial conveyance agreement by giving the President "the sole power of directing the City to be laid off in what manner he pleases," along with the right to "retain any number of squares he may think proper for public Improvements or other public uses."

The rest of the land was to be divided into lots, with the owners keeping every other lot, which would now have vastly increased value as part of the permanent capital. In addition, the proprietors would receive "twenty-five pounds per acre [$66.67 at the time] for any land taken "for public buildings or any kind of Public Improvements." They would not, however, receive compensation for streets or alleys needed.

All of the principal landholders signed the March 30 agreement, with the exception of a few who did not attend the Georgetown meetings. "Even the obstinate Mr. Burns has come into the measure," Washington wrote Jefferson jubilantly of the old Scotsman who had long stubbornly refused to sell his extensive property between the potential sites of the President's House and the Capitol.

The accord itself seemed fair enough in view of greater monetary return to be expected from private lands that otherwise would have continued as farm and woodland country. But it was also clear that Washington had negotiated a highly favorable deal for the public.

With no immediate outlay of funds, the government had acquired half of the territory that would make up the Federal Capital. Moreover, the cash and credit from the direct sale or auctioning off of its own lots would be available to finance the designing and construction of the city's public buildings.

"This business being thus happily finished," Washington confided to his diary for March 30, "and some directions given to the Commissioners, the Surveyor and Engineer . . . I left Georgetown, dined in Alexandria, and reached Mount Vernon in the evening."

He remained there until April 7, looking into problems on his estate and preparing for his next major Presidential mission—the long-planned tour through the southern states.

Riding in a gala procession that included a 12-oared barge and attending boats such as are pictured here, President Washington arrived at Charleston Harbor, South Carolina, during his extensive tour of the South in 1791. Received everywhere with acclaim, he met his most spectacular welcome in this fashionable city, where leading citizens feted him with receptions, balls, breakfasts, formal dinners, a concert, and fireworks. At the still-preserved old Exchange Building, looming in the background, Washington delivered one of the many speeches he gave on the trip. In them he often took pride in telling his hosts of his recent success in acquiring land for the new capital by the Potomac.

Pictorial Field-Book of the Revolution by Benson J. Lossing

Andrew Ellicott, a well-known professional surveyor, was hired by President Washington to mark the first boundaries of the future District of Columbia. Ellicott also prepared the first topographic map of the District, and saw it published in 1792. A member of the prominent Ellicott family of Maryland for whom Ellicott City was named, Andrew was assisted in his work at various times by his brothers Benjamin and Joseph.

Courtesy Silvio Bedini, Smithsonian Institution

Washington's wide-ranging travels through the South, like his northern tour soon after his inauguration, was arranged so he could observe for himself how people felt about their Constitutional Government of 1789 that had replaced the state-based Articles of Confederation.

In stopping at various state capitals, and meeting with individual leaders of Virginia, the Carolinas, and Georgia, he soon found that his personal popularity was as great as ever. Everywhere along the way there were parades, military escorts, receptions, formal dinners, welcoming speeches, crowded church services, musicals, and balls. At times, thousands of citizens gathered to pay him honor.

As the President and his entourage crossed rivers and raised dust along winding country roads, they encountered the usual misadventures of travel at the time. Washington also added to his own knowledge of the deeper South, as hosts at the many places where he slept proudly showed him the sights of their communities, from orphanages and newly built canals to Revolutionary battle sites.

One surprising sidelight on the human side of George Washington comes to us in seeing how the usually laconic statements in his diary brightened up with his delight in the adoration of the ladies who greeted him.

In fashionable Charleston, South Carolina, he wrote that he was "visited about 2 O'clock, by a great number of the most respectable ladies . . . the first honor of the kind I had ever experienced and it was as flattering as it was singular."

As the experiences became less singular, the number noted in his diary grew from "256 elegantly dressed and handsome ladies" to "at least 400 ladies the number and appearance of wch. exceeded any thing of the kind I had ever seen."

Less romantic, though no less pleasing to the President, was the opportunity the trip gave him to tell officials "on every proper occasion," of his successful agreement with the Potomac Valley landowners. In fact, one of his first acts after reaching Richmond, on April 13, had been to inform Governor Randolph of the progress made, and to persuade him to advance $40,000 of Virginia's promised grant of $120,000 to help construct the Federal institutions.

This pleasant glow, however, would not last. While he was still in Charleston early in May, Washington received a letter from the Commissioners enclosing correspondence in which some of the proprietors refused to sign the deeds of conveyance and title needed to carry out the original contract.

Still more painful to Washington's pride was the implication by the recalcitrant landowners that he had misled them about the amount of land that would go to the public.

Taking more territory than they expected would be required, they wrote reproachfully, "would only tend to lesson the value of the rest, without any real benefit to the public—as the price of lots would diminish in proportion as the number for sale increased. . . ."

Washington indignantly refuted the landowners' arguments in his quick response to the Commissioners from Charleston. "It is an unfortunate circumstance in the present stage of the business . . ." he said, "that difficulties unforseen and unexpected should arise to darken, perhaps to destroy, the fair prospect which it presented when I left Georgetown. . . ."

The agreement they had approved, he went on, was "alike conducive to the public welfare, and to the interest of individuals, which . . . would be most benefited by the amazing increase of the property reserved to the land holders. . . . Upon the whole," he ended his letter, "I shall hope and expect that the business will be suffered to proceed. . . ."

Eventually, of course, the business would proceed, but not until after the President returned to Mount Vernon on June 12, and again met with the proprietors and the Commissioners.

Andrew Ellicott, the competent surveyor who in 1790 ran the original boundary lines of the 10-mile-square District of Columbia, is shown at work in the field with his assistant, Benjamin Banneker. In this huge mural painting by William A. Smith—exhibited at Maryland House near Aberdeen, Maryland—Ellicott's topographic map of the District covers the broad background behind the two figures.

Mural by William A. Smith.
Courtesy the artist.

During Washington's absence in the South, Ellicott and L'Enfant had been working hard on their respective assignments of boundary surveying and city planning.

On April 15, 1791, Ellicott—accompanied by two of the Commissioners and "a large concourse of spectators"—dedicated the District's first boundary stone at Jones Point on the Potomac, near Alexandria. Time worn, and tide battered, it can still be seen there behind an old, now-deserted lighthouse.

It was a joyous occasion, however, when Ellicott laid that first boundary stone at the southern tip of the 10-mile District Square. Fully aware of the historic importance of the event, the members of the new District community put on a succession of civic activities that included a Masonic parade, many toasts to the future, and expressions of vain hope that "jealousy, the green-eyed monster" would be forever buried beneath the stone being commemorated.

L'Enfant, for his part, had eagerly used his time to explore every aspect of the region entrusted to his skill and judgment.

Day after day, on horseback and on foot, in good weather or bad, he followed his dream through the swamps, fields, and over the rolling hills of the Potomac countryside. For he had gained his heart's desire back in March, when Washington approved the rough draft of his "grand plan," as he informed Jefferson. It was, he wrote proudly, "to be done on principle conformable to the ideas which I took the liberty to hold before him. . . ."

Gradually, as he worked out the details, the outlines of a great capital came into being in the Frenchman's mind. By June 22, 1791, he had produced, and submitted for Washington's approval at Mount Vernon, a "progress map" and a long, detailed report covering "the principal points" of his plan.

Drawing on his memories of Paris—and perhaps on features suggested by maps of south European cities he knew and had requested from Jefferson—L'Enfant envisioned a metropolis of right-angle streets, overlaid by broad diagonal avenues, and enlivened by circles, squares, parks, and gardens. With the mild climate of the Potomac Valley in mind, he proposed canals for navigation, waterfalls for charm, and "play houses, room of assembly, accademies and all such sort of places as may be attractive to the learned and afford diversion to the idle."

How Washington reacted to L'Enfant's far-reaching ideas is not reported in his diary or other writings. But L'Enfant's map notes indicate that the President and his architect were in accord on many subjects, including the location and description of the city's chief public institutions.

"I could discover no one [situation]," L'Enfant wrote in his oft-quoted statement about the Capitol, "so advantageously to greet the congressional building as is that on the west of Jenkins heights which stands as a pedestal waiting for a monument. . . ."

On the other hand, he felt that less monumental treatment was required for future Presidents. Their residence should have, he proposed, "the sump-

tuousness of a palace, the convenience of a house, and the agreeableness of a country seat," in fact the precise—and modest—features it still presents.

At this promising moment in George Washington's city founding, there still remained the problem of coping with the dissident proprietors. So once more, on June 27, the President journeyed from Mount Vernon to Georgetown and called the Commissioners and the hold-out landowners to his side. And, once more, the old Washington magic prevailed.

After he had explained to the group the "State of matters and the consequences of delay . . . they readily waived their objections and agd. to convey to the utmost extent of what was required."

There was one more detail to be concluded at this meeting. "Whilst the Commissioners were engaged in preparing the Deeds to be signed . . ." Washington wrote, "I went out with Majr. L'Enfant and Mr. Ellicot to take a more perfect view of the ground, in order to decide finally on the spots on which to place the public buildings. . . ."

Having accomplished this chore, the President showed the assembled land-owners L'Enfant's map, on which the Capitol and the President's House occupy their present locations. And . . . "it was with much pleasure," he told his diary, "that a general approbation of the measure seemed to pervade the whole."

At Jones Point, Alexandria, Virginia, an abandoned lighthouse overlooks a once-important boundary stone that marked the southern limit of the new District of Columbia. On April 15, 1791, this stone was set up as the first of 40 such markers placed at one-mile intervals around the District. Andrew Ellicott, who had surveyed these boundaries as an appointee of President Washington, was a leading participant in the day's elaborate Masonic ceremonies. But the now-crumbling Jones Point marker—imbedded in the sea-wall facing the Potomac—lost its meaning in 1846 when the Virginia territory was returned to the state.

District of Columbia Public Library, Washingtoniana Division

A Tragedy of Genius

OR Pierre Charles L'Enfant, the high point of his reach for success came in the late summer of 1791.

Following his last meeting with Washington in Georgetown, after which the President returned to Philadelphia and his national duties, L'Enfant worked long and hard to correct and expand the "original" or "large" working draft of his city plan.

At the same time, he was marking off the city for future squares, avenues, and streets, buying building materials, and directing work crews. As summer days grew shorter and laborers multiplied, trees were felled, crops were harvested, brick-making kilns were built—and the first wavering outlines could be discerned for what he grandiloquently described as a capital "of a magnitude . . . worthy of the concern of a grand empire."

But Washington was becoming increasingly anxious to review L'Enfant's revised plan, and to launch the sale of lots to finance it. On August 18, Jefferson wrote L'Enfant that the President expected to see him in Philadelphia to discuss "some matters which have occurred to him . . . If you are detained by laying out the lots," Jefferson warned, "you had better not await that."

L'Enfant soon arrived in Philadelphia, where he was received by Washington on the afternoon of August 27. With him he brought—or perhaps he had sent it ahead—his new map, together with another detailed report of explanation, dated August 19, that he called a "Memoir." Together, these two documents establish for all time the scope and originality of L'Enfant's ideas.

As a practical man, as well as one of vision, he was producing a master design that not only pictured handsome public buildings rising in a city of broad avenues and charming vistas, but one that held economic and social guidance for the future.

"As matters stand," he wrote in one of the voluminous notes in his report to Washington, "the sites assigned to the Congress House and the President's palace exhibit a sumptuous aspect and claim already the suffrage of crowds of visitors. . . . Nevertheless," he continued, "it is greatly to be desired that more be done. . . . The grand avenue connecting the palace and the Federal House

OPPOSITE:

Pierre Charles L'Enfant, an idealistic Frenchman who had volunteered and fought for the American Revolution, brought a great talent and large ideas to his dream of designing a capital "worthy of the concern of a grand empire." His plan for such a city was never fully completed because of various and still mysterious factors. But in spite of the controversy that surrounded his design, and the fact that less endowed men made changes in it that were incorporated in the first engraved maps of the city, L'Enfant's original concept of the capital lives on today. No authentic portrait of L'Enfant is known, though sketchy descriptions of those who knew him provided assumed likenesses.

District of Columbia Public Library, Washingtoniana Division

will be magnificent . . . as also the several squares which are intended for the Judiciary Courts, the National Bank, the grand Church . . . But . . . other exertions are necessary . . . to enlarge private undertakings."

Among other exertions, L'Enfant proposed that "Whatever will advance mercantile interests should be pushed with the greatest activity; as the canal from the Tiber to the Eastern branch which is absolutely necessary in order to insure a speedy settlement . . . and to help convey the [building] material to the two grand edifices. . . .

"Betwixt the two edifices," he added, "the streets from the grand avenue to the palace and towards the canal will be proper for shops . . . which undoubtedly will increase in a short time to a number sufficient to meet the needs of every one."

The memoir, however, carried a portent of later troubles, ticking away like an unexploded bomb. For in it L'Enfant set himself against the President's wishes by stating his firm belief that the sale of lots should be postponed. ". . . the land will not bring a tenth part of what it will later," he argued. "Besides a sale before the general plan is made public . . . will be confined to a few individual speculators who will not be interested to improve the lots."

As an alternative, "being persuaded that money is the wheel to give motion to the machine," he suggested that the government obtain a large loan, based on the credit value of the property.

L'Enfant's suspicion of speculators would turn out to be well founded, but at the time Washington paid little attention to these doubts. Nor did he favor seeking a huge government loan. No one knew better than he that Congress was in no mood to seek outside funds to finance the Potomac-side capital, and that its rivals in Philadelphia and elsewhere stood ready and eager to take advantage of any weakness.

Thus Washington called an immediate meeting in Philadelphia to discuss with Jefferson and Madison the features of L'Enfant's plan that he had already approved, along with proposed new ones. He also indicated that he would be pleased if his Virginia associates could arrange and join a conference with the Commissioners in Georgetown in order to get on with the public sale of city lots, and to decide on other details in building the capital.

The Georgetown conference was held, beginning September 8, 1791, with Jefferson and Madison serving as Presidential delegates and consultants to Commissioners Johnson, Carroll, and Stuart.

It was a highly productive gathering. One of its most important acts was the unanimous vote by the Commissioners to name the Federal City "Washington" and the Federal District the "Territory of Columbia"—a designation later changed to "District of Columbia."

Guided by the President's preferences, the Commissioners voted against L'Enfant's suggestions to postpone the lot sale and seek instead a large government loan, as well as against the Frenchman's elaborate and expensive grand canal and waterfall system.

On the affirmative aide, the Commissioners followed L'Enfant's design by making the Capitol building the hub of the city. Streets running east and west were to be named alphabetically; those stretching north and south would have names of numbers in sequence. The broad avenues, up to 160 feet wide, would honor the states then in the Union.

The city itself was divided into four sections. Again the Capitol was the hub. Its four spokes, North, South, and East Capitol Streets, plus L'Enfant's Grand Avenue that would become the open Mall to the west, separated the quarters.

Two other interesting, but later-ignored resolutions were passed at the September 8 conference. One decreed that only houses built of brick or stone could be erected within the city. The second provided that no building could be lower than 35 feet along the avenues, but that none could rise higher than 35 feet in any other part of town. This latter regulation—introduced, perhaps, because of Jefferson's interest in keeping dwellings and towns modest in size, and streets "light and airy"—may help account for the city's longtime low skyline.

More important in meeting the President's desire to speed up their project, the Commissioners set the official date for the first public sale of lots at October 17, barely six weeks away.

In addition, they notified L'Enfant of pertinent map decisions reached at their conference, and instructed him to order 10,000 copies of his still incomplete plan "struck on the best terms, and as soon as possible" in order to have them on hand for the sale.

"The troubles which were going to disappoint L'Enfant so grievously," wrote one of his biographers, H. Paul Caemmerer, began with this map request.

At the time, however, L'Enfant made every effort to carry out the Commissioners' instructions, despite his objection to the coming sale.

While still in Philadelphia, center of the Republic's young cartographic industry, he engaged a leading French engraver, Monsieur Pigalle, to produce a copperplate of his reduced over-all plan. From it, the requested copies were to be made. Unfortunately, the undertaking failed, largely because Pigalle was unable to obtain the necessary copper for the plate.

Washington did not blame L'Enfant for the unavoidable lack of maps when the auction took place on the appointed day of October 17. He did, however, learn with "surprise and concern," as he put it, of the architect's refusal to allow the Commissioners to exhibit his general plan so that potential lot buyers could see where the properties were located in relation to future public buildings.

"He conceives," Washington remarked in a letter to Commissioner Stuart, "that the sale was promoted by withholding the general map, and thereby the means of comparison; but I have caused it to be signified to him that I am of a different opinion . . . it is much easier to impede than force a sale, as none who knew what they were about would be induced to buy . . . 'a pig in a poke.' "

More detrimental to the success of the auction than missing maps was the unseasonably bad weather. Flooding rains and chill winds not only kept would-be purchasers away, but made it hard for those who did come to inspect the available lots at first hand. Moreover, the auctioneer had to chant his sales pitch inside Suter's Tavern instead of outdoors with accompanying festivities as had been planned.

Even the presence and prestige of President Washington, Secretary of State Jefferson, and Congressman and future President Madison could not save the sale from being a dismal failure. Less than $9,000 was promised to pay for 35 lots, of which only about $2,000 was collected in cash to start building L'Enfant's "two grand edifices."

Hard on the heels of the disappointing auction came another incident that marked deteriorating relations between L'Enfant and the Commissioners. Like the map fiasco, it grew out of earlier events.

In 1790, shortly before Congress established the Federal District, young Daniel Carroll of Duddington, nephew of Commissioner Carroll and rated the richest man in the community, began building a mansion on his extensive property near the future site of the Capitol building.

By November 1791, Carroll had raised the walls and roof, and faced the problem that his house not only extended into L'Enfant's recently drawn lines for New Jersey Avenue, S.E., but that it stood on land set aside for a major public square.

Since this public use had been approved by the President as part of L'Enfant's general plan, and since the land also boasted a fine spring needed to supply fountains for the Frenchman's grand design, he notified Carroll that his half-finished house would have to be torn down.

Carroll replied that it would come down "whenever it should be deemed an obstruction in consequence of building in that part of the city." He also wrote the President giving his side of the dispute.

As the controversy heated up, and arguments and suggestions passed back and forth among those concerned—including L'Enfant, Jefferson, Madison, the President, and the Commissioners—Washington decided to seek an amicable solution.

In a letter to Carroll dated November 28, he offered a choice of two alternatives: "First, to arrest and pull down the building in it present state and raise it to the same height next spring . . . agreeably to the regulations, without any expense to you." Or, "secondly, to permit you to finish it at your own cost and occupy it six years from the present date, at which period it must be removed with no other allowance from the public than a valuation for the walls in the present state of them."

To L'Enfant on the same day, Washington sent a copy of his proposal to Carroll, together with a note giving his reason for the compromise.

George Washington is so much an American
hero that few of his compatriots spend time
recalling the details of his English ancestry.
Perhaps still fewer realize that the coat of arms
of the Washington family in England not only
goes back at least 500 years, but was copied for
the flag of his own American city, Washington,
D.C. The similarity in color and design between
the two emblems is apparent in these two
illustrations: Washington coat of arms (above)
and the District of Columbia flag.

Harper's Monthly Magazine, March 1879

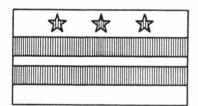

District of Columbia Public Library

Robert King, Jr., one of the talented King
family who led in District of Columbia map-
making from 1796 on, compiled this example
in 1818. Probably the first map of Washington
to be engraved and sold here, it retained many
of the features from L'Enfant's original
drawings that were taken over and changed by
Andrew Ellicott. Of interest to moderns on this
map may be the detail of Tiber Creek, which
then flowed through the center of the city from
the vicinity of Capitol Hill to Potomac outlet
close to the President's House.

Library of Congress

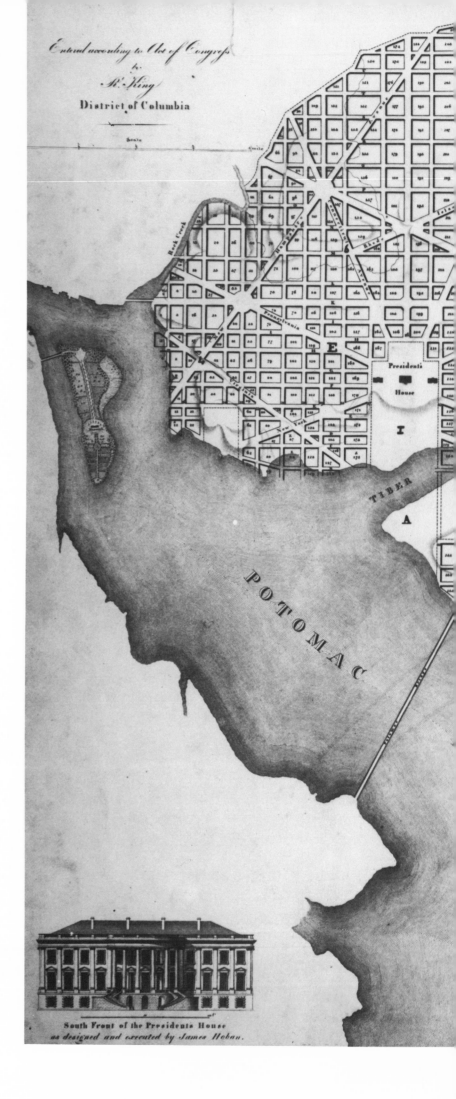

Entered according to Act of Congress
by
R. King
District of Columbia

South Front of the Presidents House
as designed and executed by James Hoban.

A Map of the CITY OF WASHINGTON in the District of Columbia established as the permanent Seat of the Government of the United States OF AMERICA

taken from actual Survey, as laid out on the ground.

by R. King
Surveyor of the City of Washington
Engraved by Chalmers Wood

[1818]

EASTERN BRANCH

Marine Hospital

Navy Yard

Capitol

East Front of the Capitol of the United States
as originally designed by William Thornton, and adopted by General Washington, President of the United States.

L'Enfant discusses his Grand Plan for the future capital with President Washington. By June 22, 1791, less than four months after his arrival in the woods and fields of the Potomac site, the French architect had prepared the first rough draft of his proposed design. In late August, he was able to show the President his corrected, though not yet complete version. Together with the maps, L'Enfant also submitted long, detailed reports describing important features of his plan—including broad, diagonal avenues, and the handsome parks, squares, and circles for which today's city has become famous.

Illustration by Herbert S. Kates from *Great Moments in the Life of Washington* by Irving Bacheller. Courtesy Grosset & Dunlap, Inc.

"As a similar case can not happen again (Mr. Carroll's house having been begun before the Federal District was fixed upon)," he said, "no precedent will be established by yielding a little ... and it will always be found sound policy to conciliate the good-will rather than provoke the enmity of any man, where it can be accomplished without much difficulty, inconvenience or loss."

Unhappily, Washington's suggestions arrived too late to halt the event that added fuel to a burning controversy. L'Enfant's patience, worn thin by overwork and pressing problems, had been exhausted by the continued delay in removing the offending structure.

On November 20, the impetuous architect-engineer dispatched an assistant, with a team of workmen, who tore down most of the building. The Commissioners were furious when L'Enfant informed them of his action only after it was well underway. In reply, they complained that even "allowing the measure to have been absolutely necessary ... our opinion ought to have been previously taken on a subject so delicate and so interesting."

The Commissioners also wrote the President that they were being ignored, and Washington sternly rebuked L'Enfant in a letter stating that he still wished him "to be employed in the arrangements of the Federal City ... But only on condition that you can conduct yourself in subordination to the authority of the Commissioners, to whom by law the business is entrusted and who stand between you and the President of the United States. . . ."

Again, Washington's instructions were not received until after the complete demolition of Carroll's house, an irrevocable incident that further increased tensions between the Commissioners and L'Enfant.

During the absence of L'Enfant on one of his trips to obtain materials to construct the public buildings—this time to buy the Aquia sandstone quarry—Commissioner Carroll had appeared at the scene of destruction and angrily ordered the workmen off the job. On L'Enfant's return to Georgetown on December 6, he at once assembled more workmen and hurried to the site, where the house was razed to its foundation.

Eventually, Carroll of Duddington would be mollified by receiving cash compensation amounting to about $4500 for the loss of his property. Since "What has been done cannot be undone," as Washington observed philosophically, the incident appeared to be closed. It seemed that peace could be restored between L'Enfant and the Commissioners.

But this was too much to expect in an undertaking of such magnitude, and one involving family connections, huge personal fortunes, and the rivalries and egos of stubborn men.

The final crisis in L'Enfant's passionate love affair with the Federal City, like the end of a Greek tragedy, was inevitable.

The new conflict was rooted in the old question of whose authority should prevail in coping with the problems of building the city.

L'Enfant was clearly authorized by the President and the Commissioners to carry on all practical details of construction, but he continued to do so solely on his own, without consulting the Commissioners' wishes.

Moreover, the specific plans and designs he was authorized to prepare for the Capitol, the President's House, and other public works, were far from being ready, though in view of L'Enfant's overwhelming workload, the Commissioners could hardly have expected such miracles of production immediately from the mind and hands of a single architect.

In any case, another and more violent altercation erupted after the Frenchman left for Philadelphia soon after Christmas, 1791, to try again to obtain an engraved map of his approved but still incomplete plan.

Before departing, L'Enfant gave written orders to his chief aide, Isaac Roberdeau, who was told to dig for building stone at the downriver Aquia Quarry.

L'Enfant informed the Commissioners of his action in a letter written just before his departure. In it, however, he merely asked for supplies and workmen needed for his program, which had been arranged without their approval or consent.

The indignant Commissioners immediately set up a conference in Georgetown and ordered Roberdeau to attend. Instead, the young man went to Aquia in accordance with L'Enfant's instructions. Whereupon the Commissioners discharged him, the overseers, and all engaged in the project.

The next scene in the brouhaha found Roberdeau rushing into the Commissioners quarters. He even "insulted them in a public and indecent manner," as he admitted in a letter to L'Enfant that same evening of January 9.

Roberdeau later apologized separately to each of the Commissioners for his conduct, but it did not save him from being arrested on a charge of trespass, and thrown into jail for a two months' stay.

Again the Commissioners wrote Washington of their mortification over their treatment. And, again Washington assured them that he recognized the necessity of their "act of authority . . . and fully approve of what you did."

L'Enfant, meantime, was still in Philadelphia and unaware of the troubles afflicting his loyal lieutenant. Mysteriously, the stagecoach mails bearing Roberdeau's frequent accounts of what was going on had failed to reach his boss.

Equally mysterious was the fact that the architect's quarters back in the Federal City would soon be entered and all of his precious drawings and papers removed—never to be recovered.

Thus L'Enfant—fired by visions of his city's coming glory—innocently took time out in Philadelphia to prepare a remarkable document for the approval of the President. Dated January 17, 1792, it covered his proposed schedule for the next five years and detailed the number of workmen needed, the cost of their labors, and of the materials to be used.

Among objectives listed were laying foundations for public buildings, digging canals, and building aqueducts, wharves, and bridges; erecting mills to saw lumber and "grind and pound plaster of paris, cement and clay."

An army of skilled and trainable men would be required, including brickmakers, blacksmiths, carpenters, stone cutters, masons, and mechanics. Their tools, provisions, and accommodations would call for everything from nails, food, and forage, to furniture, work and sleep shacks, and boats for transportation.

Virtually all equipment would have to be produced on the ground or imported, and the bill would come to a grand total, L'Enfant estimated, of $1,200,000. With about $200,000 available from the Virginia and Maryland grants, the rest would be sought through his old suggestion of foreign and other loans.

The report was a brilliant exercise in substantive and imaginative planning —but with a fatal flaw. Once more, L'Enfant bypassed the Commissioners, holding himself responsible only to the President.

There is no record that Washington ever replied to L'Enfant concerning his five-year proposal. Perhaps it was because the President was stunned by its magnitude; or perhaps because he was receiving at the same time alarming information from the usually quiet seaport of Georgetown.

There, in an atmosphere of mistrust and frustration over lagging progress on the capital project, partisans were taking sides on the known disputes between L'Enfant and the Commissioners. Some accused the Commissioners of showing partiality toward relatives in matters of land appropriations and boundaries. Others blamed L'Enfant for what they called slanderous statements about the Commissioners' ability and integrity. They even passed along unfounded rumors that L'Enfant was maliciously sabotaging surveyors' markers.

Throughout the turmoil, Washington held two firm convictions. Again and again he expressed his confidence in L'Enfant's talents and dedication to the undertaking. "... (though I do not want him to know it)," he wrote the Commissioners on one occasion, "I know not where another is to be found who could supply his place."

On the other hand, the President continued to underscore his determination to maintain the Commissioners' authority over all of L'Enfant's activities. "I . . . can only once more, and now for all, inform you," he wrote the architect, "that every matter and thing which has relation to the Federal District, and the city within it, is committed to the Commissioners . . . [and] it is from them you are to derive your powers. . . ."

But L'Enfant's time was growing short. It was already well into January, 1792, and he was making no progress in obtaining printed maps to help sell lots at the next public auction. As weeks passed, and no master engraving was available, Washington became more and more concerned.

About the middle of February, as pressures increased from L'Enfant's behind-the-scenes adversaries, the President directed that the whole engraving procedure be turned over to L'Enfant's associate-surveyor, Andrew Ellicott, who was also staying in Philadelphia during the slow winter season at the Federal City.

When L'Enfant discovered the transfer and saw the new draft, he faced Ellicott in a confrontation that caused the Frenchman to explode in a letter to Washington's secretary, Tobias Lear. He considered Ellicott's work, he said, "in the state in which it now is, most unmercifully spoiled and altered from the original plan." He had been misled, he felt, in assuming that Ellicott would not "publish the plan without my knowledge or concurrence . . . [or] without recourse to the large map in my possession."

In the same communication, L'Enfant defended himself against the charge of having neglected his assignment. He had "daily attended the progress of the business," he said, "in all its stages." Moreover, he protested, he had been deprived of essential information, in the form of a corrected ground survey in the Federal City, which he had hired Benjamin Ellicott, brother of Andrew, to carry out and forward to him in Philadelphia.

L'Enfant needed these corrections, he explained to Lear, in order to prepare his large map for the reduced version of the engraving. But again, for some mysterious reason, Benjamin Ellicott's drawing never reached L'Enfant.

Old and new evidence concerning the pros and cons of this complex map controversy are still being published today. An outstanding example is a series of articles by Richard W. Stephenson, J. L. Sibley Jennings, Jr., and Ralph E. Ehrenberg, published in the *Quarterly Journal of the Library of Congress* for its summer edition of 1979. Carefully researched, this symposium presents the latest available data in a scholarly analysis of the events and maps that raised partisans' emotions to fever pitch nearly 200 years ago.

Even then, however, it was clear that Ellicott had completed his draft for the engraving within three weeks, as Washington noted, and that the short time span would not have allowed him to develop a new design. Yet he placed his name on this draft instead of L'Enfant's—an act that Washington also noticed and mentioned in a letter to Jefferson. "The plan I think ought to appear as the work of L'Enfant," he wrote. "The one prepared for engraving not doing so is, I presume, one cause of his dissatisfication."

But L'Enfant's tragedy was not to be deviated from its course. He had still not produced the plans for the Capitol and the residence for the President. Immediate action on these major buildings was imperative lest the whole Potomac project fail. Washington took that action.

On February 11, 1792, he held a conference with his two top advisers, Jefferson and Madison, to "fix on some plan for carrying the affairs of the Federal City into execution."

What happened at this meeting was not disclosed, but it was followed by other consultations that resulted, on February 22, in a definitive letter from Jefferson to L'Enfant.

"I am charged by the President to say," the Secretary of State wrote in part, "that your continuance would be desirable to him & at the same time to add that the law requires that it should be in subordination to the Commissioners. They will of course receive your propositions, decide on the plans to be pursued ... & submit them to the President... When returned with his approbation, the Commissioners will put into your hands the execution of such parts as shall be arranged with you. ..."

L'Enfant's unhappy response to this ultimatum went on for pages and stressed his "ardent desire to conform to the judgment and wishes of the President."

At the end, however, he stated unequivocally his "determination ... no longer to act in subjection to [the Commissioners'] will and caprice. ... If therefore the law absolutely requires ... that my continuance shall depend upon an appointment from the Commissioners—I cannot nor would I upon any consideration submit myself to it. ..."

President Washington made one more effort to resolve the deadlock. On February 26, after reading L'Enfant's reply to Jefferson, he sent Tobias Lear to the architect's house to try to convince him that he could trust the Commissioners to cooperate with him.

But the situation was now hopeless. With surprising intransigence in view of his position, L'Enfant told Lear that he had "already heard enough of this matter."

The remark was a rebuff that even the long-suffering President could not tolerate. The next day, he gave his approval to a final letter from Jefferson to L'Enfant. In it Jefferson declared that since "it is understood you absolutely decline acting under the authority of the present Commissioners... I am instructed by the President to inform you that notwithstanding the desire he has entertained to preserve your agency... the condition upon which it is to be done is inadmissable & your services must be at an end."

Barely a year had passed since L'Enfant started with enthusiasm and energy on his Federal City assignment. He had created a basic design that would live on in the broad avenues and open plazas in the capital of a great and powerful nation. But, by his own decision, he had made it necessary for others to shape and suffer through the events of the next few years in the making of George Washington's city.

For his services—and his dream of that fabulous city in the sky—L'Enfant received virtually no financial compensation—again the result of his unyielding pride. At Washington's suggestion, the Commissioners offered him 500 guineas for his work, plus "a lot... near the President's House or the Capitol." L'Enfant indignantly declined the offer with an expression of "surprise" at its inadequacy.

In time, after his architectural and engineering career elsewhere had foundered again and again on the rocks of his extravagant perception of the art of the possible, L'Enfant would become a gaunt figure of poverty and misery. Forever appealing to Congress for what he believed to be his due, he eventually claimed the then impossible sum of more than $95,000.

L'Enfant died in 1825, an impoverished and embittered man, dependent for shelter and sustenance on his friends, the Thomas Diggs family of Green Hill, Maryland. He was buried there in the family plot, leaving behind a pitiful collection of personal effects that included a few books, maps, and surveyor's instruments.

In a happier epilogue to the story, L'Enfant's adopted country finally recognized the genius of the French architect and his contribution to its National Capital.

In 1909, L'Enfant's remains were disinterred from his simple, unmarked grave and transported to the Rotunda of the United States Capitol. His body lay in state there, as had those of Lincoln and others so honored.

Afterward, L'Enfant was reburied on a green hillside at Arlington National Cemetery, in a tomb surmounted by a stone table chiseled with his map of the magnificent city he never saw.

The interment of L'Enfant's remains in this impressive tomb overlooking Arlington National Cemetery came as a long-delayed epilogue to the drama that had been his life. Though President Washington continued to have faith in the talent of his city planner, he felt forced to dismiss him after L'Enfant's adamant refusal to accept supervision by the authorized Federal Commissioners. L'Enfant's career never regained its luster. When he died in 1825, he was buried in an unmarked grave on the estate of the Maryland family who had sheltered him in his impoverishment. It was not until the Centennial Celebration of the capital's birth, and the Congressional appointment of the McMillan Park Commission to look back to the city's beginnings and to plan for its future development, that a reappraisal of L'Enfant's work finally brought public recognition of his genius.
Courtesy National Park Service.
Photograph by Bill Clark

The new Western Plaza in the Nation's Capital recalls an old debt the city owes to Pierre Charles L'Enfant. Stretching along Pennsylvania Avenue for a long block, the Plaza (center) presents a huge walk-on map of the Federal City as it was envisioned by the French architect-engineer for the approval of President Washington. Designed by Architect Robert Venturi, the Plaza shows L'Enfant's plan in the form of a raised stone platform paved in contrasting white marble and dark granite, and embellished with grassy plots representing the Mall and other features of L'Enfant's imagination. In the forefront here rises an equestrian statue honoring the Polish count, Casimir Pulaski, who was killed fighting for the American Revolution.

Pennsylvania Avenue Development Corporation

CHAPTER *5*

New Start on a Rocky Road

A T THE TIME OF L'ENFANT'S DISMISSAL, the city of his soaring ambition was never further from realization. Indeed, it would not have existed at all without the stubborn efforts of Washington and his colleagues during the early years of its founding.

"I am impressed . . . with the necessity there is of carrying on this business with as much vigour as the nature of the thing will admit," President Washington wrote the Commissioners on March 6, 1792, a week after L'Enfant's firing: ". . . the whole success of the Federal City depends upon the exertions which may be made in the ensuing season towards completing the object."

In urging speed, Washington had more on his mind than the impatience of local inhabitants. In his office at the temporary capital of Philadelphia, he was constantly reminded of the never-dying hope of keeping the seat of government there. As he said in the same letter, ". . . there are not wanting those who, being interested in arresting the business, will leave no means unessayed to injure it."

Thus the most pressing "object" of the new program was to establish a solid base in the Potomac Valley by starting construction on the buildings to house the President and Congress.

To procure the necessary architectural designs in a young country with few trained professionals, the Commissioners advertised two open competitions from which to choose the best ones available.

First to win a prize—in mid-July 1792—was James Hoban, an Irish-born architect who had successfully planned the state capitol at Columbia, South Carolina. His drawing for the President's residence combined the charm of a Georgian manor house with the elegance of the classic Palladian style then popular. It was awarded $500, to be paid partly in the form of a gold medal worth ten guineas, or about $46.00.

Washington was particularly pleased with Hoban's design. On a visit to Georgetown he had joined the Commissioners in examining it and in selecting it over all others. In so doing, he rejected another interesting entry. A domed

OPPOSITE:
President Washington visits the unfinished Executive Mansion (now universally called the White House) with its architect, James Hoban. From the start, Washington devoted an enormous amount of time and thought to the construction costs and other problems of this, as well as all the other federal buildings. He enthusiastically approved Hoban's charming design for the President's House in 1792, thus assuring that the architect would win the $500 prize offered for the best plan submitted in the advertised public contest.

Painting by N. C. Wyeth for Pennsylvania Railroad. Courtesy Smithsonian Institution

Talented in many fields but an amateur in architecture, William Thornton, M.D., won $500 and a city lot for designing the United States Capitol. Washington called Thornton's plan a work of "grandeur, simplicity, and convenience." Professional architects disagreed, criticizing its lack of technical detail. The complaints were adjusted, and a compromise was reached by which a second-prize winner—a professional French architect named Stephen Hallet—received an award equal to Thornton's. The Commissioners also appointed Hallet superintendent of Capitol construction, but continuing controversy led to his dismissal.

Miniature by R. Field. Courtesy National Portrait Gallery

structure that also went back to the Italian Renaissance architect, Andrea Palladio, it was offered by an anonymous competitor who called himself "A.Z." He turned out to be the talented amateur architect, Thomas Jefferson.

The winner of the Capitol competition was another versatile amateur, Dr. William Thornton, who was born in 1759 on a small island near Tortola in the West Indies. As the son of a well-to-do-member of the Tortola Society of Friends, young Thornton was educated in England and later studied medicine at the prestigious University of Edinburgh, Scotland.

Dr. Thornton arrived in the United States in 1787, became an American citizen the following year, and settled in Philadelphia. From there he turned his lively mind to a remarkable variety of subjects, from steamboat inventions to portrait painting, novel writing, and humanitarian causes based on his Quaker associations.

When he learned of the Capitol-design competition, during an extended visit to Tortola, Thornton decided to add architecture to his repertory.

"I lamented not having studied architecture," he would write later of his bid for the Capitol prize, "and resolved to attempt the grand undertaking and study at the same time. I studied some months and worked almost night and day."

It was an auspicious moment for the brash young man to try his luck. Though the official 1792 deadline was already past, he received permission to submit a late entry because none examined so far had been considered satisfactory.

Thornton's still-unfinished sketches, submitted to Washington late in January 1793, presented a stately, low-domed building, with balancing wings for the Senate and the House. It met with instant success.

The plan "captivated the eyes and judgment of all," Jefferson commented. "Grandeur, simplicity and convenience appear to be so well combined in this plan," Washington wrote the Commissioners, ". . . that I have no doubt of its meeting with . . . approbation from you."

The Commissioners voted complete agreement on the choice, which carried an award of $500 and a city lot, but complications soon developed. First came bitter rivalry for revision and control of the winning design.

Thornton's opponent was a disappointed contestant named Etienne, or as Americanized, "Stephen" Hallet. A professional architect from France who was stranded in the United States by the French Revolution, Hallet had come close to success, as he labored on requested changes in his entry before Thornton entered the contest.

Hallet made second place, however, and, in fairness for his past efforts, was awarded a premium equal to Thornton's. To further console Hallet, he was assigned the job of making professional drawings from Thornton's appealing but impractical and prohibitively expensive plans. In addition, Hallet was appointed to assist James Hoban, after Hoban had been hired to supervise the construction of the Capitol as well as to carry out his own prize-winning design for the President's House.

With all these human factors in the situation, it was not surprising that Hallet found much to criticize about Thornton's work, and that he seized the tempting opportunity to push his own ideas in creating the form of the future Capitol.

As the dispute continued over the kind and degree of changes needed to correct the defects of Thornton's plan, Washington took a hand in resolving the stalemate that was holding up construction. "A Plan must be adopted—and good, or bad, it must be entered upon," he wrote Jefferson in a letter from Mount Vernon dated June 30, 1793.

Toward that goal, Washington informed Jefferson, he had requested Hallet and Hoban to join Thornton in Philadelphia, bringing "all the plans and documents which are necessary to elucidate the subject." Jefferson's part in the meeting would be to get everybody together, and after hearing the objections and explanations, to "report your opinion on the case and the plan which ought to be executed."

The result of this conference, which also included experienced architects

James Hoban, born in Ireland, made his fortune and his reputation as an outstanding architect in the early United States. While living in South Carolina, he designed a number of buildings, notably the state capitol at Columbia. Moving north, he added to his fame by planning the President's House. With his quiet competence and even temper, Hoban escaped the trials and rivalries that brought colleagues to grief. He remained a leader in government construction until the end of his life in 1831.

Wax portrait attributed to J. C. Rauschner. Courtesy White House Collection

as consultants, was a general agreement that Hallet's objections to Thornton's drawings were valid, but that the original ideas of Dr. Thornton should be retained as a whole within Hallet's corrected plans.

Washington was delighted with the outcome. In a letter to the Commissioners late in July, he reported that the arrangement reached would not only reduce the estimated cost by half, but that "after these opinions there could remain no hesitation how to decide; & Mr. Hoban was accordingly informed that the foundation would be begun upon the plan as exhibited by Mr. Hallet."

Meanwhile, building the President's House brought other problems to Architect Hoban, saddled as well with responsibility for erecting the Capitol.

Tools and materials were as limited as was the money to pay for them. Transportation by water was slow and uncertain. Skilled workmen were scarce, since slave labor in the region tended to keep wages down and discourage artisans from other areas. It was hard to find a stone mason who could cut a column, complained Jefferson, whose taste ran to classic column architecture.

Yet Hoban, whose unruffled competence contrasted sharply with the ambitions and jealousies of his colleagues, managed to be ready for the cornerstone laying of the Executive Mansion on October 13, 1792.

President Washington, occupied by national affairs in Philadelphia, was not present for the ceremonies. But members of the officiating Masonic Order, together with the Commissioners, Hoban, and enthusiastic fellow citizens, made the occasion a festive one of parades, rituals, and speeches.

Curiously, it appears that only one contemporary account of this important gathering exists today. We owe that report to an eyewitness in the Federal City who sent his description of the event to a friend in Charleston, South Carolina. The Charleston *City Gazette* printed an excerpt in its issue of November 15, 1792.

Reading this article today, just as it appeared at the time, gives us more than a footnote to history. It offers a quick object lesson in the eighteenth-century custom of writing "f" for "s." On the "13th inft.," the *City Gazette* reported, "the firft ftone was laid in the fouth-weft corner of the prefident's houfe. . . ."

The location of the first cornerstone of what we now call the White House has never been definitely pinpointed in the southwest corner. During President Truman's reconstruction of the house from 1948 to 1952, he directed that its foundation should not be disturbed in order to remove and inspect the stone "to satisfy curiosity."

More spectacular and better publicized than the launching of construction at the Executive Mansion was the laying of the Capitol cornerstone nearly a year later on September 18, 1793.

As the President of the Republic, and acting Grand Master of the officiating Grand Lodge of Maryland, Washington lays the cornerstone of the United States Capitol on September 18, 1793. A member of the Masonic Order for many years, and himself past Worshipful Master of Alexandria Lodge 22, Washington wears the symbolic costume of Freemasonry. The exact location of the cornerstone is still unknown, though it is believed to be in the southeast corner of the building's first-constructed North Wing.

Mural by Allyn Cox. Courtesy
Architect of the Capitol

Washington was the star of the performance as President of the United States, past Worshipful Master of Alexandria's Masonic Lodge 22, and Acting Grand Master of Maryland's Grand Lodge, under whose auspices the traditional Masonic parade and rites were conducted.

The ceremonies began on the Virginia side of the Potomac and picked up steam after the President and his military and civilian escort were ferried across the river from Alexandria to Georgetown.

Greeted by artillery salutes and joined by the first contingents of Freemasons in their symbolic aprons and insignia, Washington led the parade along the narrow dirt lane that was then upper Pennsylvania Avenue.

At the President's Square, the procession halted to take on the city's top officials, including the Commissioners and the Mayor, and to add more lodges to the parade.

With the newcomers came the Masonic Order's leading officers: Treasurers carrying jewels; Wardens, Deacons, and Stewards holding their emblems of power; Sword and Bible Bearers, and the chosen members charged with transporting the corn, wine, and oil for the cornerstone rites.

They marched "in the greatest solemn dignity," an observer would report in the *Alexandria Gazette*, "with music playing, drums beating, colours flying and spectators rejoicing." All went well until the gallant paraders reached Tiber Creek, near the foot of Capitol Hill. Forced there to break ranks and teeter across the shallow stream by stepping stones or fallen logs, men and regalia finally regrouped for the big moment at the hilltop Capitol site.

The leaders and bit players in the spectacle took their place in ritual formation. Cannon boomed and watchers hushed, as Washington, wearing appropriate Masonic costume, lowered the mechanically suspended cornerstone onto the silver plate that recorded the date and other details of the event.

"The ceremony ended in prayer, Masonic chanting Honours, and a fifteen volley from the Artillery," reported the *Alexandria Gazette*. "The whole company retired to an extensive booth, where an ox of 500 pounds' weight was barbequed, of which the company generally partook. . . . Before dark the whole company departed with joyful hopes of the production of their labor."

No one was more hopeful, or more helpful, than Washington in pushing the embryo capital toward reality by the Congressional deadline of 1800.

In letter after letter to the Commissioners and others, he devoted an extraordinary amount of time and thought to planning both large and small details of construction.

"The public buildings in size, form and elegance," he wrote, "should look beyond the present day. [But] I would not have it understood from hence that I lean to extravagance."

Thus the President, while approving an Executive Mansion that many felt went far beyond the needs of the Republic, also vetoed the proposal of a third story in the interest of economy.

Since the Commissioners met only monthly, Washington urged them to put "the affairs of the Federal City . . . under the immediate direction of a judicious and skilful superintendent," one who would reside in the city and give constant attention to its affairs.

In confidence, he mentioned the faults and possible scandals involving men handling public money, and warned the Commissioners "to act with caution in all your contracts" with building contractors permitted to carry out public works.

In the midst of leading the new nation along an uncharted political course, Washington even took the time to consider the expense and availability of workmen and materials with the same concern that a property owner might give to building his own home.

"I am convinced of the expediency of importing a number of workmen from Europe," he wrote the Commissioners in December 1792. "The measure has not only economy to recommend it, but is important by placing the quantity of labor . . . upon a certainty for the term for which they shall be engaged."

In the same letter, Washington suggested certain foreign countries, particularly Germany, from which indentured workers might be recruited. He also dealt with such mundane matters as rates of pay and the competency required of skilled artisans.

If the Commissioners agreed with his idea, he continued (knowing that they invariably did), he pointed out that "no time should be lost . . . and if you have not contemplated a proper character for this business . . . I will endeavor to obtain one . . . to go over to Germany, and a merchant also to furnish the vessel at the time and place that shall be agreed upon between them."

Yet in spite of all the sensible advice and practical support that Washington provided, work progressed slowly at the Federal City.

The second public sale of lots, in October 1792, had proved to be a second failure in bringing out the needed cash and credit. So was the third auction, held September 17, 1793, on the eve of the Capitol's cornerstone celebration. Arranged to take advantage of the presence of crowds whose enjoyment of the festivities was expected to promote enthusiasm for buying lots, it turned out to be another disappointment.

It was now painfully clear that other methods must be devised to raise funds that would keep the city project going. In this effort, the big-time real-estate speculators then ranging the country for opportunities to develop new areas were more than willing to cooperate.

Even in the days when elaborate ceremonies and formal speeches marked official functions, the Masonic rites and regalia that accompanied the Capitol's cornerstone laying offered a rare spectacle. The procession, which had begun after Washington and his entourage crossed the Potomac from Virginia, proceeded through Georgetown to the Capitol Hill site. Along the way, more and more members and officers of local lodges joined the parade. Wearing the traditional sashes and aprons, carrying emblems of Freemason leadership in Jewels, Sword, and Bible, they marched, the Alexandria Gazette *reported, "in the greatest solemn dignity, drums beating, colours flying. . . ."*

Wash drawing by Benjamin Latrobe. Courtesy Alexandria-Washington Lodge No. 22, A.F. & A.M., Alexandria, Virginia

CHAPTER 6

In Search of Rainbow Gold

SAMUEL BLODGETT, AN ENTERPRISING BUSINESSMAN who had moved from New Hampshire to Boston to Philadelphia, became the first of the rich and roving speculators to hunt gold at the end of the Potomac Valley's rainbow. He began by buying up blocks of lots early in 1792, and by the end of the year had accumulated properties that would soon include nearly 500 more acres extending from what is now Dupont Circle.

Full of great expectations in fields ranging from architectural designing to national economy and education, Blodgett applied for, and received from the Commissioners, the post of building superintendent suggested by Washington. But no sooner had he embarked on his new job, in January 1793, than the irrepressible entrepreneur persuaded his bosses to back his project for a real-estate lottery. Its main prize would be a $50,000 Great Hotel in the heart of town, to be designed by the distinguished architect James Hoban.

At first the lottery seemed to be a good idea. The government would benefit by the building of a fine hotel and other structures demonstrating the growth of the city. Blodgett, who was charged with responsibility for selling the majority of the 50,000 tickets, would gain through his real-estate holdings, since some of his lots and houses were among the prizes. For these he could claim whatever price he wished to deduct from cash returns.

The lottery winners, too, were expected to be happy. Except for such expenses, all of the money collected was to be paid out in prizes.

It didn't happen that way. The number of ticket purchasers, sought throughout the country, fell far short of hopes. Building programs failed, and the announcement of winning numbers was delayed until late in 1794, more than a year after the first drawing.

By that time, both the public and the Commissioners were disenchanted. Blodgett's assignment as superintendent had not been renewed when it expired in January 1794, and Washington had expressed his disapproval of Blodgett's conduct in a letter to one of the Commissioners. "... his appointment did not in my judgment answer the end ... contemplated," Washington wrote. "...

OPPOSITE:
Before it was finished, Samuel Blodgett's "Great Hotel" (far right) was offered as first prize in one of his flamboyant lottery schemes. As a successful businessman from the north, Blodgett had begun speculating in Federal City real estate in 1792. He invested heavily in desirable property, and soon obtained a civic post as supervisor of public buildings. He then embarked on his lottery adventures, which resulted in the loss of his official job, and eventually in his financial ruin and a stay in debtors' jail. Blodgett's Great Hotel, located at 8th and E Streets, N.W., was not completed until after 1800. The winner of the lottery never received his award, and the building was never used as a hotel. It served various purposes, and was occupied by the United States Patent Office when it burned in 1837.

Watercolor by Nicholas King. Library of Congress

James Greenleaf, member of a rich Boston family and admired as a bright, young financier, arrived at Georgetown in 1793 with a letter of introduction from President Washington to the Commissioners. He came at an auspicious time when funds were low and investors were needed to speed lagging construction of public and private buildings. Greenleaf was permitted to buy up thousands of city lots on highly favorable terms. And from then on—until he was temporarily incarcerated in a Philadelphia debtors' prison—he became the center of a tangled financial and legal web unequaled in the history of the Nation's Capital. This curious situation can be understood today only in the context of the time, a period when the young Republic was the happy hunting ground of speculators who bought, mortgaged, and sold vast expanses of land with the patriotic goal of developing the country—and adding to their own wealth.

Watercolor, 1793. *Greenleaf and Law in the Federal City* by Allen C. Clark

It appears evidently enough now, that speculation has been his primary object from the beginning."

Nevertheless, the optimistic promoter was soon launching another lottery, this one without official support. Blodgett's "Federal Lottery No. 2," offered in the summer of 1794, promised as its first prize a mansion valued at $30,000, followed by other prizes of lesser worth.

The results satisfied no one, least of all the lottery contestants for drawings that were never held, or the "winners" whose house prizes were unfinished, and sometimes nonexistent.

The winner of the half-built Great Hotel took his case to court to gain the full value of the building as represented in lottery advertisements. He won his suit, and Blodgett lost everything when he was forced to forfeit his remaining real estate in the Federal City to pay off the deed of trust given as security.

Blodgett's downfall would be complete in 1802. After failing ventures elsewhere finally folded, he was sentenced, under the harsh laws of the period, to serve time in a Philadelphia debtors' prison.

Yet, even there, he arranged a deal whereby his good friend, Dr. Thornton, signed a $10,000 bond permitting him to take short walks outside the prison walls for his health. He kept walking on one such occasion, leaving Thornton to make good the bond, and Blodgett somehow at large.

The ambitious spinner of financial fantasies was then a broken and discredited man. In his remaining years he was reduced to soliciting small public contributions to build a monument to George Washington, and to establish a national university in the Capital City. It is recorded that Blodgett raised $7,000 for the university project, which had long been close to his heart, as it was to Washington's. But whatever happened to these and other funds he collected remains lost in his fabulous manipulations.

Back in the summer of 1793, when Sam Blodgett had been riding high on the road to ultimate ruin, an advance member of a new set of even richer land speculators appeared on the Potomac Valley scene.

James Greenleaf, a 27-year-old Bostonian who was already active in national and international finance, arrived in the Federal City bearing a letter of introduction from the President to the Commissioners.

In it Washington informed them that Greenleaf wished to build a number of houses, "provided he can have lots upon such terms & conditions as may correspond with his interest . . . He has been represented to me as a Gentleman of large property and having command of much money in this Country & in Europe," said Washington in recommending that the Commissioners "listen with attention & weigh with candour any proposals that may . . . promise the growth of the city." But he "could say nothing," he pointed out with his usual caution, "from my own knowledge."

Robert Morris was a name to conjure with in the early 1790's when the Federal City was coming into being by the Potomac. Revered as the financier of the Revolution who had raised desperately needed funds during the darkest days of the struggle, he was now considered the richest man in the country and known to be a close personal friend of the President's. With Morris as a partner in James Greenleaf's purchases of huge amounts of property in the future capital, Washington and his Commissioners were confident that the operation was sound. Yet within five years, the speculators' seemingly safe operation had collapsed, and Morris had joined Greenleaf in the same debtors' prison.

Engraving by Phillibrown after Alonzo Chappel. New York Public Library

The Commissioners were doubtless impressed with the young man's look and credentials, and perhaps even more by his land-development association with Robert Morris. Famous as the financier of the Revolution, Morris was reputed to be the richest man in the country and known to be a long-time friend of Washington's.

Greenleaf also had the advantage of timing in his proposals. The till for constructing the public buildings was almost out of funds. The sale of city lots had been lagging, and the prospect of money in hand, as well as more houses to fill the open spaces of the Federal City, was highly appealing to the Commissioners.

Thus Greenleaf was allowed to buy 3,000 District lots at the minimum rate, but with the requirement that ten houses must be built every year until 1800, and that for every third lot sold, a house would be raised within four years. In addition, he agreed to pay $2,200 each month in the form of a personal 6-percent loan to be used by the Commissioners for Federal construction.

The initial purchase of 3,000 lots was increased to 6,000 within a few months when Morris, who had previously been a silent partner, joined Greenleaf as a principal for the expanded deal.

Soon another rich and powerful financier named John Nicholson became a third partner in the syndicate. Nicholson, who held the important political post of comptroller-general of Pennsylvania, was not only a personal friend of Morris's, but a business associate who brought to their affairs the prestige of owning millions of acres of land in Pennsylvania and other states.

Together, during the next several years, these three men would dominate the Federal District's real-estate market, while maintaining homes and other enterprises elsewhere.

In the beginning, they paid their bills to the Commissioners on time, started the promised housing construction, and added constantly to their lot purchases. No one suspected then that after the syndicate's involuntary departure, there would be left behind a maze of clouded titles and individual-and-group machinations that have baffled historians and lawyers ever since.

Certain details of the trio's operations stand out today as examples of the truism that the only sure thing in the pursuit of boundless fortune is uncertainty.

Since credit formed the basis of the syndicate's growing land acquisitions, Greenleaf needed a huge loan to put money down on these lots, as well as to keep up with his already committed debt to the Commissioners.

In 1794, he planned to borrow the grand sum of $1,200,000 from banking institutions in Holland, the center of European finance. Lacking cash to pay in full for the property titles required to negotiate such a loan, he persuaded the Commissioners to make an exception of this rule. With Washington's approval, and with the glittering hope of the much-needed foreign loan dangled before their eyes, the Commissioners transferred titles to 2,000 city lots with no more security than the personal bond of the syndicate.

Greenleaf himself had excellent business and personal connections in Amsterdam, where he had earlier served as United States Consul, and where he had married the Baroness Scholten, daughter of a prominent Dutch family.

But times had changed. Money was scarce as a result of disrupted economies and social unrest brought on by the French Revolution and the spread of Napoleonic wars. Holland's moneymen turned down Greenleaf's requested loan. Though later negotiators for the syndicate obtained a smaller sum, it amounted to only $120,000, a tenth of what was desired and needed. Even this credit was swallowed up by the voracious paperwork of the syndicate; the Federal City gained no benefit from it.

During the next two years, the careers of Greenleaf, Morris, and Nicholson went up and down with the happenstance of luck and events.

Greenleaf, always on the alert for buyers to take the unproductive Potomac lots off his hands, found two rich customers on one of his frequent stays at his New York City residence. Both were Englishmen—Thomas Law and William Duncanson—who had recently arrived from London.

Law was the brother of an English lord and in his own right an accomplished veteran of administrative service in India. His friend Duncanson was a highly successful businessman looking for new fields to conquer.

Greenleaf charmed the two men into visiting the Federal City, where they were so captivated by the prospects of the future National Capital that they bought large blocks of land for speculation, and decided to make their homes there.

Law purchased 500 lots, Duncanson about half as many. Law was more canny in protecting his investment by obtaining mortgages in an equal amount from Greenleaf. Duncanson failed to take this precaution, and would eventually pay the price by losing the fortune tied up in his lots.

Law won more than property interests by settling in the Federal City. As a glamorous widower, he met and wooed Eliza Custis, Martha Washington's vivacious 19-year-old granddaughter, half his age. They were married in March, 1796, and spent their first months together in what came to be called Honeymoon House, at Sixth and N Streets, S.W.

Meanwhile, the $200,000 in cash that Greenleaf collected from Law and Duncanson had gone the way of the $120,000 from the Dutch financiers. The Commissioners received none of it to meet the mounting indebtedness of Greenleaf and the other members of the syndicate.

But nothing could now save the group's paper empire, over-extended in various states, and under-supported by solid foundations. At every turn, their efforts failed to shore up credit, or to secure more funds to pay off their commitments, taxes, and interest.

The last months of the syndicate's existence were marked by acrimonious and often publicized disputes between the members; by threats from the Commissioners of legal suits against them; and by forced sales of their more or less worthless notes and other paper promises.

The inevitable crash came in the summer of 1797. A few months later, Greenleaf was confined to a Philadelphia debtors' prison, from which he would emerge after about a year by pleading bankruptcy.

Robert Morris, once seemingly invincible, joined Greenleaf early in 1798 in the same prison, where he would remain for more than three years. During one Thanksgiving-holiday season, George Washington visited his old friend, and dined with him and his family in a prison room set apart for the occasion.

Nicholson shared the same fate and Philadelphia jail of his colleagues in 1800. He died there the following December, leaving a widow and eight children, and owing more than four million dollars.

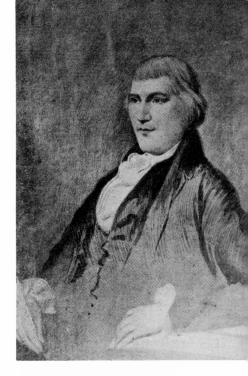

John Nicholson, who became the third partner with Greenleaf and Morris in the Federal City's real-estate deals, brought equally impressive credentials to their activities. As the Comptroller-general of Pennsylvania, and holder of millions of acres of land in Pennsylvania and elsewhere, Nicholson appeared as solid a citizen as could be imagined. But nothing could have rescued the syndicate's shaky credit-based empire, further weakened by economic dislocations of the time. Its final crash in 1797 ended all benefits to the city, though the group's machinations did produce a few blocks of houses that would help ease the problems of the government's transfer from Philadelphia. Nicholson himself, like his colleagues, landed in the Philadelphia debtors' prison. In 1798 he died there.

Painting by Charles Willson Peale. *Greenleaf and Law in the Federal City* by Allen C. Clark

There was even a duel to add more drama to this frantic period. William Duncanson found himself so hopelessly entangled in the affairs of the failing syndicate, and so frustrated at his inability to extricate himself, that he challenged Greenleaf to meet him on a dueling field.

The result, however, was more comic opera than tragedy. The cap in one of the pistols snapped harmlessly, and the whole thing was called off.

The final collapse of the syndicate's golden bubble was felt throughout the credit institutions and building operations of the Federal City. But it came as no surprise. Signs of trouble had been apparent as early as the summer of 1795, when the group failed to pay the regular installments on its obligations.

At that time, President Washington and his three newly-appointed Commissioners—Gustavus Scott, Dr. William Thornton, and Alexander White—obtained a $20,000 bank loan based on the Commissioners' private credit. From then on, it was up to them to find more and better sources of funds.

It would not be easy. The Commissioners said it all on one occasion, after it was suggested that they inaugurate a system of sewers for the city. They agreed that such drains were essential. "But set to build a city without funds," they wrote dolefully in answer, "what can we do?"

CHAPTER 7

A Promise Fulfilled

As WORK ON THE PUBLIC BUILDINGS limped along by fits and starts, the appearance of various business undertakings marked the gradual development of private enterprise.

By the mid-1790's, a number of wharves and warehouses were ready to help move trade and building supplies along water routes that were the natural highways of the region. Factories were turning out such products as sugar, beer, and barrels, and businessmen had set up offices to deal in these and other commercial articles.

Here and there, taverns and hotels had opened their doors to patrons from near and far, including a stream of distinguished foreign visitors, curious to inspect the new Republic and its capital in the making. A post office was set up, and the town's first newspaper, called the *Impartial Observer and Washington Advertiser*, began printing in the spring of 1795.

More houses, too, built in rows or spaced along future streets, were giving a settled look to certain areas, though woods were everywhere. "Excepting the streets and avenues, and a small part of the ground adjoining the public buildings," one foreign traveler remarked in 1796, "the whole place is covered with trees."

Still, persistent efforts were being made to get on with the city's development. In that same year, the Commissioners notified Farmer Burns, who had been raising crops on his widespread fields between the Capitol and the President's House, that he could no longer sow his seeds there. The reason? They were preparing to cut a passageway through the swampy expanse near the foot of Capitol Hill in order to open up the lower stretch of Pennsylvania Avenue.

Foremost among the local real-estate developers was Thomas Law, Washington's relative by marriage, who was known to be a dynamic and brilliant—if somewhat eccentric—fellow.

Law owned considerable land in the Federal City, most of it situated around the Capitol and south to the Eastern Branch waterfront, where he firmly believed the city would grow and expand.

Thomas Law was one of the few big land speculators who struck it rich in the Potomac Valley. An already wealthy Englishman with a distinguished career in colonial India behind him, Law came to the United States in 1794. He was introduced to the prospective capital by promoter James Greenleaf, and so impressed was Law by what he saw that he not only bought his first 500 lots from Greenleaf, but decided to make his home there. He also took a bride from the area—Eliza Parke Custis, the lively young granddaughter of Martha Washington. Law was more successful in investments than in his marriage, which ended in an early separation and eventually in divorce.

Greenleaf and Law in the Federal City by Allen C. Clark

After moving from their Honeymoon House to their new residence on New Jersey Avenue, S.E., the Laws lived in high style, entertaining often and lavishly. It was not destined to last. Washington had disapproved of the match from the beginning, largely because of the couple's age difference. And, in fact, the marriage would turn out to be a turbulent one, ending eventually in the rare solution of divorce.

When the Laws first separated, gossip said that Eliza had run away with a young army officer. Her husband denied the rumors and later underscored his feelings by willingly paying the generous maintenance sum promised in their marriage agreement.

The citizens of the growing village by the Potomac, however, had more to worry about than personal gossip. First of all there was the question of whether the Federal buildings would be ready by 1800 to meet the needs of the government on its transfer from Philadelphia.

During the last two years of his presidency (which would end on March 4, 1797), Washington and his Commissioners made heroic efforts to find loans that would make the hope and obligation possible.

They appealed to the Bank of the United States, and to banking institutions in Amsterdam and London. Nothing came of it. European financiers were suspicious of the new Republic with its odd notions of equality and its embryo capital in the woods. Even if they had been willing to take a chance, the same chaotic conditions that had blocked Greenleaf's pursuit of loans made money totally unavailable.

As a last resort, Washington was forced to seek help from the Congress—a step he had long avoided as a sign of fatal weakness that would encourage still-unreconciled rivals to press their claims to the permanent capital.

He presented his petition to Congress in January 1796, in the form of a Message from the President. With it went a "Memorial" from the Commissioners citing the advantages of government support for its National Capital.

Reassuringly, Washington did not request a direct appropriation. Instead, he asked only for permission to use city-owned property as security in making loans for the public works. As an extra precaution, he also sought a guarantee that the United States Treasury would reimburse lenders for any loss resulting from default.

These were hardly unreasonable favors to expect from a Congress that had founded the city and was soon to move its headquarters there. But the House and Senate debated for four months before passing the desired resolutions.

With this backing, however grudging, Maryland was persuaded to lend the District $100,000 in United States stock at 6-percent interest. In return, the Commissioners were required to give the state two security bonds—one in their official capacity for the amount of the loan, and the other as individuals for twice as much.

And there was still another catch. The stock's market value proved to be only about 80 percent of its $100 par value, leaving the city with that much less to bank on.

Besides lack of money and of a sufficient force of trained workmen—who were to be found neither at home nor abroad—the Commissioners had other problems to contend with. Disputes between Capitol architects and superintendents led to disruptive incidents and firings. Quarrels between dissatisfied landowners and the Commissioners themselves added to the confusion and to loss of essential time.

Yet somehow both public construction and private enterprise inched ahead. President Washington selected the sites for the Treasury, State, Navy, and Post Office buildings during a visit to Mount Vernon in the fall of 1796. He placed them near the President's House, and thereby started a controversy in which opponents maintained that the executive departments should be closer to the Capitol.

In any case, Washington's choice stood, though actual building operations were delayed for many months, apparently because of the President's belief that the Capitol should take precedence over all other Federal buildings in readying the city for the National Government.

"It may be relied on," he wrote the Commissioners in his last important communication before the end of his final term, "that it is the progress of that building, that is to inspire, or depress public confidence.... It would gratify the public wishes and expectations;—might possibly appease clamor ... [if] the Capitol is in such a state of forwardness as to remove all doubts of its being ready for the reception of Congress by the time appointed."

The last spurt of building activity exploded in 1798. It was sparked partly by the government's approaching arrival, and partly by increasing confidence in the future of the Potomac Valley, following another epidemic of yellow fever in Philadelphia. This was the third time that the scourge had struck the city in recent years, and its effect was a thorough dampening of public enthusiasm to retain the capital in Philadelphia.

More financial support, too, became available at this time for Federal construction. The United States Congress provided a loan for $100,000, while Maryland voted another loan in the same amount.

Most of the new private construction sprang up near the Capitol and near the President's House, where the need was greatest to provide shelter and sustenance for incoming members of Congress and officers of the executive departments. Hence hotels, taverns, and homes doubling as rooming houses made up the bulk of almost magically appearing structures.

Notable among these buildings was a hotel going up at First and A Streets, N. E. One of Thomas Law's numerous projects, it was backed by a personal loan from Washington that showed in this practical way his keen concern over the expected housing shortage.

Eliza (or Elizabeth, sometimes called Betsy) Custis Law was the eldest of four children fathered by Martha Washington's son, John Parke Custis. Shortly before Eliza's marriage to Thomas Law, she was described by then Vice President John Adams as "a fine, blooming, rosy girl." She became more than that in her first year as wife and hostess in the growing Federal City. She presided over one of the most elegant households in town, entertaining with lavish hospitality. Behind the fashionable front, however, trouble loomed. Law soon returned to England for a visit, and gossips whispered that glamorous Eliza paid too much attention to gallant young officers in the vicinity. The divorce came in 1810, following a long separation.

Portrait by Ellen Sharples. Museum and Art Gallery, Bristol, England. Courtesy Frick Art Reference Library

First section of the Capitol building to be completed, the Senate Wing was about ready for occupancy when Washington died in December 1799. Within six months, the whole government would begin its transfer—bag, baggage, and records—from Philadelphia to its permanent home. Since no other shelter was available for other federal establishments, the 32 Senators shared their boxlike North Wing with 106 Representatives, along with members of the Supreme Court, Circuit Court, and the Library of Congress.

Watercolor by William R. Birch. Library of Congress

At this point, Washington was once more a private citizen, happy to be home at his Mount Vernon estate. But whether as President or country squire, he would never cease working for the success of his Federal City.

All during his presidency, he had stopped regularly at Georgetown on frequent trips to and from Mount Vernon. As he checked on progress being made in creating the future capital, it seemed that there were always problems which only he could resolve.

His very presence was a promise of achieving his goal. And, in response, the people of the area turned out in force on every possible occasion to show their gratitude, admiration, and respect for him.

The most spectacular of such festive gatherings was the spontaneous demonstration that greeted General and Mrs. Washington on their last homecoming from Philadelphia at the end of his final term.

On the couple's arrival at the Federal City on March 14, 1797, crowds welcomed them with an artillery escort that delivered a burst of cannonfire at the Capitol site. A little later, a sixteen-gun salvo boomed another salute as Washington passed the unfinished President's House to the huzzas of the assembled citizens.

Between honors that day, Grandmother Washington and the General dined with Eliza and Thomas Law at their residence on New Jersey Avenue. Later they moved across town to stay overnight at the northwest home—on K at 26th Street—of Eliza's sister Martha ("Patsy" Peter), who had also married a prominent builder named Thomas Peter.

In thus dividing his time between the Custis sisters, Washington was following the long-established pattern of his many visits to Georgetown and the Federal City. It was one that doubtless gave him pleasure. But it meant more than sentiment to this most visible and hard-working booster for the city. The fact that Martha Washington's granddaughters were married to successful promoters was a living symbol of their—and his—faith in the permanence of the Potomac Valley site.

Moreover, Washington himself owned considerable real estate in the city. At the public sale, back in September 1793, he had bought four lots near the Eastern Branch. The following day, as he later informed the Commissioners in seeking information about his properties, he had arranged to purchase four more in the rival northwest area, lest "it should be believed that I had a greater predilection to the southern, than I had to the northern part of the City."

Then he added, with characteristic modesty, "I had no desire at that time, nor have I any now, to stand on a different footing [as President] from any other purchaser."

Five years later—in September 1798—Washington went a step further in his efforts to prepare the capital for the incoming administration of President John Adams.

In his now private role, he acquired another large lot on North Capitol Street. There he began erecting two houses with a common front that would permit their use as a double or single dwelling.

He engaged the popular architect-physician Thornton to draw up several plans for the buildings. For their interior, however, he laid out his own floor design to include eight bedrooms for each house, several garret rooms, and a general-use ground floor. He also planned a separate kitchen, linked to the main structures by a covered walkway like that at Mount Vernon.

From then on, Washington's ambitious project brought endless headaches to a man perennially land-poor and short of ready cash to pay running expenses.

In letters to Dr. Thornton, the Commissioners, and to George Blagdin—his construction boss—he poured out a litany of delayed performance and rising costs that would be painfully familiar to any house builder today.

Blagdin's estimated price for his proposed houses, Washington complained, "far exceed any aggregate sum I had contemplated. . . . Eight or at most $10,000 was the extent of my calculations. . . ."

Instead, the contract finally signed put the amount at $11,250, with Washington to accept the burden of supplying the "painting, glazing, and iron mongery."

Handling these and other finishing details took enormous time in nego-

This sketch of the twin houses that Washington began build-ing near the Capitol in 1798 closely follows his own descrip-tion of how he wanted them to be. "I saw a building in Philadelphia of about the same dimensions . . . that pleased me," Washington wrote his architect, Dr. William Thornton, designer of the Capitol. It consisted, Washing-ton continued, "of two houses, united Doors in the center, a Pediment in the Roof. . . ." In another letter to Thornton, he indicated that he wished his houses to be "three flush stories in Brick, besides Garret rooms." And in still another communication to the archi-tect, Washington explained his basic purpose in engaging in this enterprise. "To aid in the accommodation of the members of the General Government," he wrote, "was my only inducement to these buildings."

Drawing by Geraldine Linder

tiations, correspondence, and frequent visits to see how the houses were pro-ceeding.

Unexpected costs, too, frustrated the master of Mount Vernon, who was accustomed to free or inexpensive labor and materials needed there. He could not understand, for example, how "a well little more than 30 feet deep" could bring a bill "upwards of £ 70," and he suspected that Blagdin's charges, when "not enumerated in the Contract [were] pretty smartly whipped up."

As months passed, Washington was forced for the first time in his life to borrow money from a bank at "ruinous interest."

Yet work went on, despite disappointments and setbacks. As the two houses neared completion, he proudly described them to a prospective tenant as "not costly but elegantly plain. . . ." They are "capable of accommodating between twenty & thirty boarders," he said, "in the judgment of those better acquainted in these matters than I am."

The remark expressed Washington's own belief that his property would help meet the demand for housing in the vicinity of the Capitol. Indeed, a letter to Thornton soon afterward underscored the point. "To aid in the accomodation of the members of the General Government," he observed, "was my only inducement to these buildings."

Washington would not live to see his fine houses occupied. Nor was either the President's House or the Capitol more than barely habitable when he died on December 14, 1799. Much of the interior of the Executive Mansion was still unplastered then, and only the North Wing of the Capitol—future head-quarters of the Senate—was completed.

But the task that Congress had entrusted to President Washington ten years before had reached fulfillment. Within six months of his death, the national seat of government would find its permanent home beside the Potomac.

To Washington, during the final years of the struggle, the future of his city looked bright. In writing to Sally Fairfax, love of his youth, he pointed out in May 1798 the many advantages of the new capital. "A century hence," he said, "if this country keeps united (and it is surely its policy and interest to do it), will produce a city, though not as large as London, yet of a magnitude inferior to few others . . . [It has] a situation," he continued, "not excelled for commanding prospect, good water, salubrious air, and safe harbour, by any in the world. . . ."

What remains today of the little settlement that Washington knew? Not much, as growth and development programs have uprooted the past.

Scattered over the great modern capital that he foresaw are a few sturdy buildings from the late eighteenth century. The Laws' Honeymoon House, for one, still stands in the Southwest. In Georgetown, which became part of the National Capital in 1878, another interesting example is a row of handsome residences that raise their roofs high along Prospect Avenue, so named for its commanding view from these Potomac bluffs.

The Old Stone House, also in Georgetown on an extension of Pennsylvania Avenue now called M Street, has long been a tourist attraction. There is an unsupported tradition that Washington once used this odd little building as his headquarters in planning the Federal City.

This theory may have grown out of another doubtful tradition that it was a base for city-planner L'Enfant, or one of the offices of the Commissioners who worked with Washington on the Federal City project. Historians, however, do not question the eighteenth-century origin of the Old Stone House or its value as a relic of pre-Revolution architecture. They agree that it was built in 1765, and that Washington must often have passed it on his way between Georgetown and Mount Vernon.

Still another historic structure—this one in the heart of town—has become newsworthy in recent years, not for its past but for its future.

We know this small, unobtrusive building at 15th and F Streets, N.W., as Rhodes Tavern. Its construction was begun in 1799 by a brick manufacturer named Bennett Fenwick. Two years later, Fenwick had rented his three-story house to innkeeper Williams Rhodes, whose name and fame would be linked henceforth with his tavern.

As the oldest building in downtown Washington, D.C., Rhodes Tavern has played a part in many important areas of capital life, both civic and private. At present, however, it is the prize in a tug of war between a group of ardent preservationists and powerful developers bent on either destroying it, or, if necessary, on moving it to another location away from its historic associations.

At this writing, the future of Rhodes Tavern, unlike its past, remains uncomfortably uncertain.

OPPOSITE:

Restored as a Historic House Museum in the 1950's, the Old Stone House in Georgetown is perhaps the oldest remaining building in the Nation's Capital. It was erected in 1765-66, and is valued by historians and architects as an interesting example of pre-Revolution architecture. The Old Stone House has a fascinating story as a witness to, and sometimes a participant in, the early growth and development of the little port of Georgetown into a flourishing business and social center. This building has been under the jurisdiction of the National Park Service since 1953.

District of Columbia Public Library, Washingtoniana Division

This modern painting of Rhodes Tavern is based on a watercolor made by Baroness Hyde de Neuville in 1817. The Baroness, who was the wife of the French Minister, lived across the street from the tavern. Today, Rhodes Taven, which was begun in 1799 at 15th and F Streets, N.W., is the last remaining structure between the White House and the Capitol that dates from Washington's lifetime. It stands also as the first, though unofficial, town hall of the growing city. During the War of 1812, Rhodes briefly sheltered some of Britain's invasion forces.

Painting by Earl Minderman, Bethesda, Maryland. Courtesy of the artist

"MY OWN VINE
AND FIG TREE"

Tribute to a Man

OWERING OVER ALL OTHER REMINDERS of George Washington's time stands a symbol of his strength and integrity more eloquent than a thousand words.

The first thing a visitor sees on approaching the Nation's Capital is the white shaft of the Washington National Monument. Reaching toward the sky, this obelisk-shaped monolith is as stark as the Pyramids and as instantly recognizable.

Washington never saw it, of course. The cornerstone was consecrated on July 4, 1848, by the Grand Master of the local Masonic Lodge in the presence of thousands of witnesses. Among them was Martha Washington's grandson, George Washington Parke Custis, President Polk, and a then little-known Illinois Congressman named Abe Lincoln.

It took 40 more years of alternate progress and delays before the obelisk was completed and finally opened to the public in 1888, during the administration of President Cleveland. Since then this marble tribute has represented to Americans and the world the solid and noble character of the first President of the United States.

But there is still another memorial, not far away, that shows a different side to Washington. For those who would touch the heart and life of the man himself, the road leads past Alexandria in Virginia, with all its memories of George and Martha, and on to Mount Vernon—his "own vine and fig tree."

To see the estate in perspective, one should take to the air, a view that would surely have enchanted its eighteenth-century proprietor.

Looking down on this jewel-like scene, etched in green and white along the banks of the Potomac, it is easy to understand George Washington's passionate pride of possession.

"No estate in United America is more pleasantly situated than this," he once said. "It lyes in a high, dry and healthy Country . . . on one of the finest Rivers in the world . . . in a latitude between the extremes of heat and cold."

OPPOSITE:
Of all the memorials raised to George Washington since he became America's hero, none is as spectacular as the Washington National Monument in the city named for him. Under trouble-plagued construction between 1848 and 1888, "The Monument," as it is simply called, lifts its starkly beautiful shaft 555 feet high against the sky. It is the first thing the visitor sees on approaching the city. Various civic events take place there throughout the year, and on the Fourth of July the annual fireworks celebration draws thousands of spectators.

Washington National Monument Association. Photograph by Donald J. Crump

From above you can see, too, how like a small village Mount Vernon was, with its shady lanes, central bowling green, and work and living quarters scattered around the stately manor house.

"The General has . . . everything within himself," a guest of 1785 reported, "carpenters, bricklayers, brewers, blacksmiths, bakers. . . ."

In writing a fellow Virginia farmer, the master of all this once observed that "the life of a Husbandman . . . is honorable. It is amusing and with judicious management, it is profitable."

Certainly Washington found his greatest personal satisfaction not in his successful military career or as President, but in developing and perfecting his home and farm.

He began expanding Mount Vernon's modest eight-room dwelling in 1757, a few years after acquiring it through the death of his half brother Lawrence. He strengthened its foundations, raised it from 1 1/2 to 2 1/2 stories, and added a new kitchen, an office, and other "dependencies," or service buildings.

In his first year as the head of a family, young Washington discovered his talent for, and delight in, the art of farming. He invented a cultivating plow, and "found she answered very well."

Soon he was corresponding with English agriculturists, and experimenting with imported European plants as well as with domestic crops. He bought "do-it-yourself" books, including one called *A New System of Agriculture, or a Speedy Way to Grow Rich*.

As the Washingtons settled down to placid domesticity, George repaired and enlarged his old outbuildings and added more—a storehouse, washhouse, smokehouse, dairy, and spinning and weaving shops producing linen, cotton, and woolen cloth.

At times, several hundred people, whites and Negroes, lived and worked in the bustling community that was Mount Vernon. Over its domestic side presided Martha—a plump, kindly mistress, whose modesty and housekeeping abilities would long obscure her other qualities of steadfast courage, shown during the Revolution, and her poise and grace as First Lady.

Bit by bit, Mount Vernon's modest manor house changed and grew from the time George Washington acquired it in 1754, following the death of his half brother Lawrence. To this dwelling in the honeymoon spring of 1759, Washington brought his bride, Martha Dandridge Custis—widow of Daniel Parke Custis—and her two children. From then on, Mount Vernon would remain the lifelong home of George and Martha Washington. It was the place to which he returned with joy, and which he constantly improved and added to—even while he was leading the Revolution and serving as the nation's first President. Between 1774 and 1776, he directed, often from the war front, the building of the south wing (at right here), which would house his library and provide another bedroom. Begun, too, in 1776, was the north wing (left), whose construction dragged on until after the Revolution. In 1787 came the mansion's crowning touch, a weather vane in the shape of a dove of peace. By Washington's express order, the olive branch in its beak was painted green.

Courtesy The Mount Vernon Ladies' Association of the Union

1757

1759

1774

1775

But even in the earlier years, the family house was growing too small for comfort as Washington's increasing prestige brought more and more guests.

In the spring of 1775, the master was engaged in building the first of two additional wings when he was called to the Revolution.

It was not easy to leave such an important construction job. For Washington, like other property owners of his day, was his own architect. He planned structures by books and examples, then kept a sharp eye on the contractors, or "undertakers," as they were known, who carried out the work.

Thus even from the war front, General Washington sent frequent directives to his manager and relative, Lund Washington.

"The chimney in the new room [at the north end] should be exactly in the middle of it—the doors and everything else to be exactly answerable and uniform," he said in one letter. "Hasten the undertaker," he warned in another, "otherwise you will have it [the addition] open I fear in the cold and wet weather."

The new south wing was basically complete as early as the fall of 1775, while the General was encamped outside British-held Boston, trying to hold an army together. Work on the north wing, however, to provide a much-needed dining and reception hall dragged on and on.

Meantime, Washington had no intention of neglecting his crops and lawns. He wrote Lund long, explicit instructions on just what and where to plant, and in return expected detailed regular reports.

In a letter dispatched from New Windsor, New York during the uncertain period before the battle of Yorktown, he wistfully asked for home news: "How many Lambs have you had this Spring? How many Colts are you like to have? . . . Have you made good the decayed Trees at the ends of the House? . . . Have you made any attempts to reclaim more Land for meadow?"

Yet Washington's love for his estate did not keep him from sharply rebuking his caretaker when he was informed that Lund had taken provisions from Mount Vernon aboard an enemy warship prowling the Potomac.

"It would have been a less painful circumstance to me," the General wrote sternly, "to have heard . . . they had burnt my House, and laid the Plantation in ruins."

1776

1778

1785

1787

The Marquis de Lafayette chats with General Washington, his commander from the Revolution, during a visit to Mount Vernon in 1784. Mrs. Washington's youngest grandchildren, Nelly and George Washington Parke Custis (offspring of her late son, John Parke Custis) play on the veranda and on the lawn. Little Nelly is seen clinging to her grandmother's knee. Washington and Lafayette were old friends, much like father and son in their relationship. Twelve years later, Lafayette's own son, named for George Washington, made a similar visit to Mount Vernon.

Print from painting by T. P. Rossiter. New York Public Library

The Washingtons spend a pleasant evening with Martha's grandchildren, Nelly and George Washington Custis. These youngsters were taken to live permanently at Mount Vernon after the death of their father, John Parke Custis, at the end of the victorious Yorktown campaign. The two older girls, Eliza and Martha, remained with their mother, who later remarried. Washington treated all of his children and grandchildren by marriage —whether outside or within his immediate household— with the same warm affection. He gave them gifts and solid advice on their lessons and love affairs, as well as on other problems that inevitably arose.

Painting by John Ward Dunsmore. Courtesy Fraunces Tavern Museum, Sons of the Revolution, New York

The British spared Mount Vernon itself on their plundering foray, but Washington found much to do on his return. Moreover, skilled workmen were hard to find.

"I am a good deal in want of a House Joiner and Bricklayer," he wrote a Baltimore friend, on learning that a shipload of indentured servants had arrived. "If they are good workmen, they may be of Asia, Africa, or Europe. They may be Mahometans, Jews or Christian of an(y) Sect, or . . . Athiests."

Gradually, however, despite setbacks, and despite the eight long years he devoted to the demanding duties of the Presidency, Washington made Mount Vernon into one of America's leading country seats.

By the time of his final retirement to a serene and busy life here, he had added four more farms to his original holdings—increasing his tidewater land from 2,000 to more than 8,000 acres.

His gardens were show places, his fields flourishing. He operated shad and herring fisheries, bred livestock, and milled his own wheat into fine flour that sold as far away as England and the West Indies.

At the mansion, guests found fashionable green-painted wallpaper and Venetian blinds. They admired the imported English flagstones that floored the stately pillared porch, the ornamental shrubs and trees, the serpentine roads, and deer park.

Characteristically, Washington chose for the crowning touch to his house a weather vane in the form of a dove of peace. ". . . how much more delightful" he wrote an English correspondent in 1788, "is the task of making improvements

Two fine gentlemen (left) watch as Washington shames them by helping to put out a fire during a visit to Alexandria in 1799. Washington had been an honorary member of the town's Friendship Fire Company since it was organized in 1774. That same year, when he was in Philadelphia for the Continental Congress, he inspected the equipment used there, and purchased a small fire engine that Alexandria still exhibits proudly to the public.

Harper's Monthly Magazine, February 1880

on the earth, than all the vain glory which can be acquired from ravaging it, by . . . conquests."

But as long as Washington lived, Mount Vernon would grow and change. On the day before his death, he tramped through fresh snow, marking trees to be replaced in extending his riverside lawns.

It was only afterward that decline set in.

Martha Washington survived her husband by less than three years. In the spring of 1802, she was entombed beside him in the old family vault at Mount Vernon.

Under Washington's will, his five Potomac farms were divided among various heirs, the family house and 4,000 acres going to his nephew, Bushrod Washington.

In turn, Mount Vernon passed to Bushrod's nephew, John Augustine Washington; then to his son, young John Augustine.

By that time, decreased acreage and depleted soil had made farming unprofitable. Worse, the cost of maintaining the estate under the pressure of unavoidable guests and sightseeing hordes was pushing the owner to the verge of ruin.

The situation seemed hopeless. Both the Federal Government and the State of Virginia refused to buy the property. And Washington refused to turn it over to private speculators for exploitation.

Then came an oddly fateful incident.

CHAPTER 2

A Lady Finds a Mission

THERE WAS A FULL MOON one fall night in 1853, when a Potomac steamboat passed Mount Vernon. As the bell tolled the traditional salute to the first President, a woman passenger going home to South Carolina looked out toward the shabby old house.

"I was painfully distressed at the ruin and desolation of the home of Washington," Mrs. Robert Cunningham wrote her daughter Ann the next day. Why should not "the women of his country . . . try to keep it in repair," she asked, "if the men could not do it?"

To Ann Pamela Cunningham, her mother's idea gave new meaning to life. Thrown from a horse in girlhood, this sensitive, red-haired young woman had since been a semi-invalid living on the family plantation, Rosemont, in western South Carolina.

Now, despite continuing pain from the old spine injury, she flung herself into a campaign to purchase Mount Vernon as "a monument of love and patriotism."

She made her first appeal for funds through an open letter in the Charleston *Mercury* of December 2, 1853. Addressing it "To the Ladies of the South," she signed it "A Southern Matron," in deference to the Victorian code that respectable women did not flaunt their names in public.

Increasing interest in the project, however, soon forced Miss Cunningham to shed anonymity and broaden her sights.

Gradually she set up an organization called the Mount Vernon Ladies' Association of the Union. To give it national scope and prestige, she invited influential women, one from each state, to serve on its board of vice regents which she headed as regent.

The system proved spectacularly successful. Contributions began pouring in from all parts of the country, and as far away as the Hawaiian Islands. Donors included New York newsboys and West Point cadets; actor Edwin Booth, author Washington Irving, and President James Buchanan.

OPPOSITE:
To Ann Pamela Cunningham, a gentlewoman of South Carolina, the nation owes the preservation of Mount Vernon as George Washington knew it. Her project began in 1853, when she learned of the sorry state of the old house and hoped to remedy it. The first phase ended in 1858, after she had rallied women from all over the country to her cause, and raised enough money to buy the estate from its last Washington-family owner. Today, Mount Vernon is still owned and run by Miss Cunningham's Mount Vernon Ladies' Association of the Union. It uses the entrance fees collected from visitors to maintain the estate and add to ever-increasing furnishings and ornaments of the early-American period.

Courtesy The Mount Vernon Ladies' Association of the Union

The stoutest support came from Edward Everett—educator, statesman, and popular orator, who was destined to make the forgotten main speech when Lincoln spoke the few immortal words of the Gettysburg Address.

To save Mount Vernon, Everett delivered 129 benefit lectures and wrote 52 newspaper articles. His total contribution amounted eventually to $69,064, more than a third of the understood purchase price.

Meantime, John Washington had decided not to sell, even after the Ladies' Association offered to raise the money and present the estate to Virginia as a national shrine.

So Ann Pamela Cunningham made the slow, painful trip to Mount Vernon in 1856, to "charm the bear," as she wrote later.

Mr. and Mrs. Washington entertained their guest politely, but were about to send her away in miserable defeat when another providential accident changed the course of history. She missed the return river boat.

While waiting for the next one, Miss Cunningham made a last desperate plea. This time she won Washington over to her side. "I held out my hand—he put his in mine . . ." she described her triumph, "our compact was closed in silence."

There were still legal and legislative problems to solve, but finally on April 6, 1858, Mount Vernon's last private owner signed a contract to accept $200,000 in installments for the old Washington home and 200 acres of land. Moreover, the property was to go directly to the Association, to be restored and preserved as decided by 31 dedicated Ladies in 31 States.

The Washington Family moved out in the spring of 1860, turning Mount Vernon over to the Association's first superintendent, Upton Herbert, a descendant of the Fairfaxes who were George Washington's neighbors.

Left behind by the departing family were priceless gifts: the bust of General Washington made here in 1785 by French sculptor Jean Houdon; the big world globe that Washington had used in his study; and a key to the fallen Bastille of Paris, presented to him by Lafayette as "the main key to the Fortress of Despotism."

It was a promising start whose bright hopes soon darkened. Miss Cunningham, who had guided developments by correspondence and visits to the estate, returned to her South Carolina home in December 1860, for what she thought would be a short stay. She was at the Rosemont plantation when Charleston guns opened fire on Fort Sumter. The Civil War exploded, and the Association's First Lady was trapped for the duration.

Fortunately, Ann Cunningham had left in charge of Mount Vernon her new secretary—a young woman from Troy, New York, who was as courageous and capable as she was charming.

Tiny, demure Sarah Tracy, her black hair pinned up in neat braids, kept the estate an island of peace through the war. After Union forces occupied

OPPOSITE:
A decaying shell of what it once had been, Mount Vernon's Mansion House stands forlornly on its hill in the days before Ann Cunningham and her Ladies wrought their miracle. Ever since the Civil War, this organization has carried out a series of restoration and reconstruction programs that have gradually turned the declining estate into a handsome showplace of the life and times of an eighteenth-century country squire.

Courtesy The Mount Vernon Ladies' Association of the Union

nearby Alexandria in May 1861, passing soldiers often stopped to make the tour, stacking their guns outside the gates. When they could, they paid the small fee asked to help meet modest supply and repair costs.

Important persons came too. Mrs. Abraham Lincoln "and a select party of friends," as a Washington newspaper put it, made the boat trip in March 1861. Sarah Tracy, who had been away at the time, reported in a letter to Miss Cunningham that Superintendent Herbert gave the visitors "a little lunch of bread, butter and '*Ham.*'"

Later that year, when Prince Napoleon of France and his suite suddenly rode up in two carriages, hostess Tracy mustered the French she had studied, and "ordered *everything we had to be cooked.*"

The Prince was impressed with Mount Vernon's odd situation, she noted —"a little corner of earth . . . kept sacred, neutral ground."

Yet the war often seemed terrifyingly near, especially when the vibration of cannon at the battles of Bull Run and Chancellorsville could be felt.

Occupation by Federal troops once threatened Mount Vernon itself, driving Sarah to seek out Commander in Chief Winfield Scott at Washington. "God bless the ladies," murmured the General to an aide, and gave his word that no military forces would be sent to Washington's home.

From Scott, Sarah also obtained a pass to carry mail, and sell produce and buy supplies. Then came a stiffer blockade, and officers who questioned even Scott's signature. So stubborn Sarah risked sentry fire on bypaths to Washington, and rewon her precious pass through President Lincoln.

In Mount Vernon's archives, modern students find this and other Civil War stories preserved in a yellowed collection of Sarah Tracy's letters.

From the last few we learn that she stayed on for several more years, busy with duties she called "comically diversified," from mending and marketing to fishing and raising flowers for sale.

"I have made with my own hands over 800 bouquets," she wrote, "which has paid for the superphosphates, farm tools, etc., and we have nearly enough to put a new zinc roof on the Tomb."

Thus the rickety old house and grounds were slowly being reclaimed when Miss Cunningham returned late in 1866. Reluctantly she agreed to the resignation of pretty Sarah Tracy, who would later marry faithful Upton Herbert and live happily with him on another Virginia plantation.

Frail Ann Cunningham took over the double task of personally maintaining and rehabilitating the estate. Despite failing health, she stuck it out until 1874, leaving an eloquent appeal for the future in her Farewell Address that is still read aloud at the Association's annual meetings.

"Ladies, the home of Washington is in your charge. . ." she said. "Let no irreverent hand change it; no vandal hands desecrate it with the fingers of progress . . . though we slay our forests, remove our dead, pull down our

churches, remove from home to home . . . let them see that we know how to care for the home of our hero."

Since then, successive regents have kept to the letter and spirit of these words. They have rebuilt and renovated as if this were a real community with real inhabitants. Like detectives, they have traced the Washingtons' possessions to descendants, friends, and museums. By purchase, gift, and loan, they have filled the mansion with articles whose only difference from those in other homes is that nothing here wears out, and everything is linked with the life and time of George and Martha Washington.

For Mount Vernon is not just a memorial to a hero; it is the recreated hearthstone of a family. When you step from the rushing twentieth century into this serene early-American world, it is not hard to fancy yourself a guest of the Washington family.

CHAPTER 3

Mount Vernon Lives Again

START AT THE WEST, or courtyard, entrance to the charming country house. Its exterior walls are sheathed in what Washington called "rusticated Board," cut and beveled to imitate then-popular European masonry.

Beyond the brown-painted door, bearing its original brass knocker, you walk into a broad central passage that reaches across the house to the piazza, facing the river.

In this pleasant, roomlike area, now refurnished with black horsehair Federal chairs (some of which the Washingtons once used), Mount Vernon's host and hostess greeted perpetually flowing streams of visitors.

Here came military and civilian leaders, American and foreign, to seek the advice of the famous retired general.

Here came three future Presidents, Jefferson, Madison, and Monroe, who would follow Washington in the "Virginia Dynasty."

Here, too, came former comrades-at-arms, curiosity seekers, and European notables bearing letters of introduction. One Englishman, a young artist and architect named Benjamin Henry Latrobe, left a graphic record of his stay in the summer of 1796.

Latrobe, who would later become the third Architect of the United States Capitol, described Washington as "uncommonly majestic and commanding," and, moreover, a man who enjoyed "a humorous observation." He found Martha unaffected and good humored, and her granddaughter, Nelly Custis, more beautiful and intelligent than he had "conceived consistent with mortality."

Latrobe also sketched the house, grounds, and members of the household, which then included Lafayette's young son, George Washington Lafayette, sent to America to escape the horrors of the French Revolution. One pencil study of Washington was returned to Mount Vernon only in 1963.

From the mansion's central passage, modern visitors look into four rooms that saw 40-odd years of Washington's social and family life.

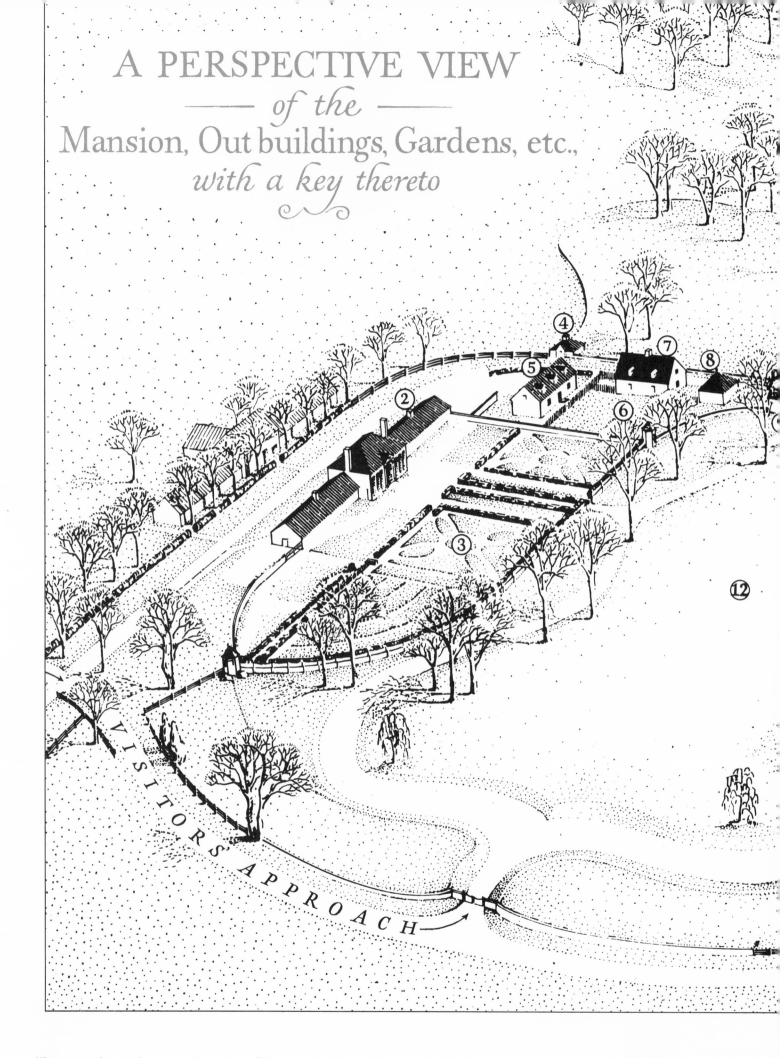

A PERSPECTIVE VIEW
of the
Mansion, Out buildings, Gardens, etc.,
with a key thereto

VISITORS' APPROACH

"*It's astonishing what a number Of small houses the General has . . . for his Carpenters, Bricklayers, Brewers, Blacksmiths, Bakers," a visitor wrote about Mount Vernon's facilities in 1785. This chart of the estate as it has now been restored explains what Washington's guest meant.* Courtesy The Mount Vernon Ladies' Association of the Union

1. Mansion
2. Greenhouse and Quarters
3. Flower Garden
4. Icehouse
5. Museum

Tomb & Wharf →

6. Botanical Garden	11. Courtyard	16. Laundry Yard	21. Paddock
7. Spinning-House	12. Bowling Green	17. Washhouse	22. Park
8. Storehouse	13. Kitchen	18. Coachhouse	23. Potomac River
9. Gardener's House	14. Butler's House	19. Kitchen Garden	24. Vineyard Enclosure
10. Office	15. Smokehouse	20. Stable	

Christmas dinner with the Washingtons at Mount Vernon brings on the usual good food and good conversation. Many guests who sat at this table wrote glowingly of both. One recalled an impressive menu of "roasted pigg, boiled leg of lamb, roasted fowls, beef, peas, lettuce, cucumbers, artichokes, etc., puddings, tarts, etc. etc." For drinks there was a choice of wines, beer, or cider. It was then the custom to serve dinner in mid-afternoon, tea at six, and supper, if desired, at about nine.

Painting by Oliver Kemp, Century Magazine, vol. 55. New York Public Library

Above the mantel in the West Parlor, you see a pastoral scene, the "neat landskip" he ordered from London in 1757, before his marriage. On another wall hangs his portrait copied from one painted by Charles Willson Peale in 1772. In his British (Virginia Regiment) uniform, a half smile touching his lips, Colonel Washington appears at the peak of vigorous, handsome maturity.

Mrs. Washington's tea service, set up in the West Parlor, like Nelly's open harpsichord in the adjoining Little Parlor, or Music Room, hints at lively parties in the old house.

Washington enjoyed music, though he once said he could "neither sing one of the songs, nor raise a single note on any instrument." Long an ardent dancer, in later years he liked to watch the young people from the door, slipping away quietly if his presence dampened the fun.

The downstairs bedroom across the hall invites repose, with its fourposter bed and comfortable furniture, its red toile spread and matching curtains. In days of country hospitality, many a traveler must have welcomed the haven.

Indeed, Washington and his wife could seldom enjoy a meal without the company of either casual or invited guests.

"Unless someone pops in unexpectedly," he wrote one day in 1797, "Mrs. Washington and myself will do what I believe has not been done within the last twenty years—set down to dinner by ourselves."

As restored with many original pieces, the Small Dining Room is one of the most attractive spots in the house. Chippendale ladder-back chairs and two small tables all belonged to the Washingtons. Some of the same pictures that hung here have come back, as has the handsome silver-plated wine cooler that was used at Philadelphia and later at Mount Vernon. A table setting of fruits, nuts, and wines reflects the menu that was served one of the Washingtons' guests in 1798.

Highly ornamental ceiling and elaborate mantel give this room an elegant air. More down to earth is the square mahogany chest that stands in the corner. It contains a number of surviving bottles for wine and spirits that Washington bought in 1760, together with the chest, and for which he felt he was badly overcharged at a price of some 17 guineas.

"Surely, here must be as great a mistake, or as great an Imposition as ever was offered by a Tradesman," he wrote indignantly to his London agent. "The case is a plain one, and such as I could get made in this Country . . . for less than four Guineas."

Between afternoon dinner and tea, and at night by candlelight, Washington often retired to his study in the south wing.

He answered his mail, and kept his accounts and diaries at the secretary-desk in this spacious, cheerful room. His wall bookcase again holds many of his books on history, farming, biography, military campaigns—even poetry. Nearby stands his world globe. His fowling piece rests against the wall in the corner.

To Washington, his study was also his private chamber, a use that is pointed up by the presence of his personal dressing table. On it rests a small copper washbasin, a substitute for the one he actually used for his morning ablutions.

The most imposing room in the mansion, however, is the Large Dining Room, 16-feet high and stretching the length of the north wing. From the Revolution's battle front on Harlem Heights, in September 1776, Washington instructed his manager, Lund Washington, to see that the new addition was "executed in a masterly manner." And so it was—after 12 years, when the last detail of lavish stucco and wood decoration was finally completed.

A strange story (probably apochryphal) clings to the carved and inlaid marble mantel you see here. It had belonged to the English estate of Samuel Vaughan, who visited America and became Washington's admirer and friend. After the Revolution, Vaughan had the mantel shipped from London as a gift to embellish Mount Vernon. Enroute, pirates were supposed to have hijacked the ship's cargo and landed with it at a West Indies port. From there, someone mysteriously sent the mantel on.

Better documented are other incidents concerning the mantel which reveal

At this secretary-desk, which returned to Mount Vernon in 1905, Washington conducted his private and public affairs during the last few years of his life. Here he recorded the day's events in his diary, made entries in his account books, gave instructions to his farm overseers, and wrote long, personal letters to family and friends. Here, when engaged with official and military assignments for his country, he reached final decisions on crucial action to be taken by the government, and dispatched orders and suggestions to others that would affect the destiny of his and other nations.

Courtesy The Mount Vernon Ladies' Association of the Union

OPPOSITE:

As a family man without children of his own, Washington lavished affection on Martha's children and grandchildren. This late nineteenth-century painting of the General and Mrs. Washington's youngest granddaughter, Nelly Custis, reveals something of her beauty that led young men to express extravagant sentiments of admiration. Wrote the dashing Polish patriot, Count Julien Niemcewicz, after a 1798 visit to Mount Vernon, "She was one of those celestial beings so rarely produced by nature, sometimes dreamt of by poets and painters, which one cannot see without a feeling of ecstacy. . . ."

Painting by Howard Pyle. *Harper's Monthly Magazine*, November 1896

an interesting sidelight on Washington's taste as reflected in his choice of simple, sturdy furniture for his home.

When he received this fine gift in 1785, he was naturally pleased to have it, but he remarked in thanking his friend Vaughan that it was "too elegant and costly by far I feel for my room, and republican stile of living. . . ."

Even later, after the master of Mount Vernon had added many other attractive features, visiting Benjamin Latrobe was struck by the contrast between the magnificent mantelpiece and the rest of the furnishings.

"This is the only expensive decoration I have seen about the house," he wrote in his journal of 1796, "and is indeed remarkable in that respect. Everything else is extremely good and neat."

As you climb the old staircase that felt Washington's step, you pass duplicates of the original English engravings that Washington bought in Philadelphia during his Presidency. Then you peer into six bedrooms that hold eighteenth-century washstands, chests, and beds with handmade covers.

Not all of these articles were here in Washington's day. But many have returned, and all the others have been chosen by careful research in old docu-

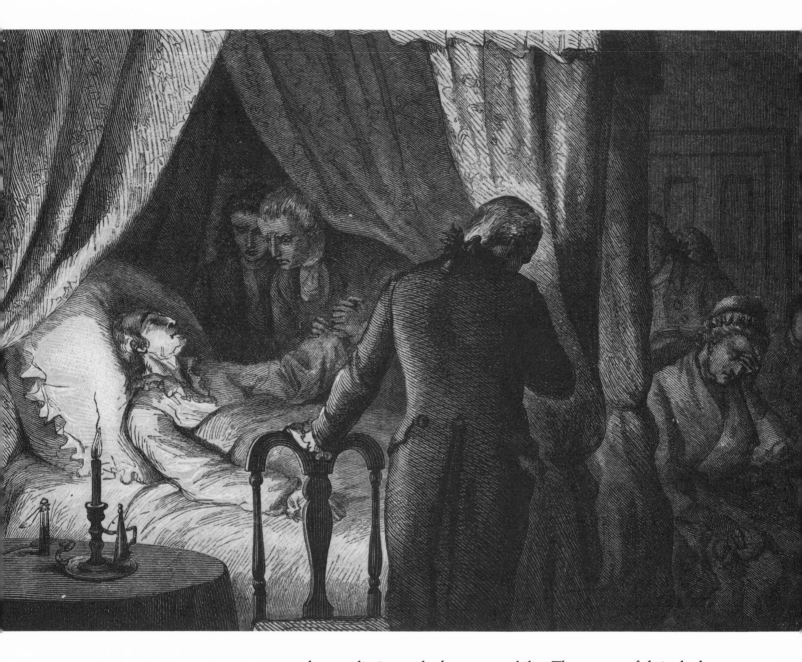

ments, letters, diaries, and other memorabilia. The most useful single document of the kind, say staff members, was the executor's inventory of Washington's estate, prepared soon after his death.

The narrow bed and chest in the little hall bedroom off the upper passage are in keeping with a letter suggesting that young George Washington Parke Custis occupied such a room. The painted woodwork in the Yellow Room was restored according to microscopic analysis of original paint chips, as were all rooms at the mansion. The papered, then-painted walls and decorative borders were based on contemporary records.

Moreover, many priceless objects on the second floor have immediate ties with Washington and his family. The chest of drawers in the Yellow Bedroom, for one, is documented as a piece he bought for Mount Vernon before he was married.

OPPOSITE:
George Washington died on this four-poster mahogany bed that was restored to Mount Vernon by family descendants in 1908. Present during his last illness was his old friend and chief attending physician, James Craik, together with two consultants, Drs. Gustavus Brown and Elisha Dick. Present, too, was his faithful secretary, Tobias Lear. Later, Lear would write a detailed account of Washington's brief illness, after exposure to snow and sleet, and report on the emotion-filled deathbed scene of December 14, 1799. "... About ten minutes before he expired (which was between ten and eleven o'clock)," said Lear, "his breathing became easier and he lay quietly ... he expired without a struggle or a sigh...."

Illustration by F. O. C. Darley. *Our Country* by Benson J. Lossing

In the Lafayette Bedroom, where the Marquis once slept, you find Martha's trunk, "pack'd by her own hands," says a faded letter pasted in the top, when the time came during the Revolution for her annual trip to join the General in his winter quarters.

This letter was written long afterward by Martha's eldest granddaughter, Eliza Parke Custis Law, to *her* grandchildren. In it, Mrs. Law recalled her distress when her "Sainted Grandmother" left, "& oh how joyfully when she returned did I look on to see her cloaths taken out & the many gifts she always brought for her grandchildren."

In the Nelly Custis Room you can see the very crib, canopied with white netting, in which lay Nelly's and Lawrence Lewis's first child. A baby girl, she was born here late in November 1799, only days before George Washington's death.

Most important of all Mount Vernon relics are those restored to the bedchamber and dressing rooms used by George and Martha Washington. Back in place is Mrs. Washington's French writing desk and dressing table. One of his campaign trunks, leather covered and with a name plate engraved "Genl. Washington 1775," stands at the foot of the bed.

It was on this huge bed, between tall mahogany posts, that Washington died—obeying "the summons ... with a good grace," as he had expressed the hope in a letter written only a few months before.

After Washington's death, Martha closed up their second-floor bedroom, and moved to this small attic chamber from which she could look out on the hillside tomb that held her husband's remains. Her gloomy vigil ended with her own death in the spring of 1802, when she was buried beside him in the family vault. Washington's 8,000-acre Mount Vernon estate, which had been left to Martha for her lifetime under the terms of his will, now passed to various members of the Washington clan. In time, as the process of division and subdivision continued, only the nucleus of the deteriorated house, subsidiary buildings, and the surrounding land remained of the flourishing community so carefully tended by George Washington.

Illustration by A. J. Keller. *Harper's Monthly Magazine,* December 1899

CHAPTER 4

Visiting Memory Lane

BUT VISITORS LIKE TO REMEMBER the living man, and nowhere is that memory more pervasive than under the great shade trees he planted, and in the gardens he watched grow and flourish.

Count Niemcewicz, a Polish guest in 1798, described these gardens as "perfectly kept . . . in English style. All the vegetables indispensable to the kitchen were there," he noted. So were berries—"currants, raspberries, strawberries, gooseberries—a great quantity of peaches and cherries . . . very many beautiful trees: the tulip tree with flowers like the tulips . . . magnolias with flowers whose scent is almost as strong as the smell of an orange tree."

Mount Vernon's master grew orange trees, too, along with lemons, and other delicate plants kept inside his greenhouse in winter. This big, brick structure facing the flower garden was the estate's finest outbuilding. Destroyed by fire in 1835, it was reconstructed in 1951 from original specifications and archeological study.

Slaves once lived in the greenhouse wings, furnished now with double bunks and simple articles of daily life. Washington owned hundreds of slaves, but deplored the practice on both moral and economic grounds.

"I wish from my soul," he wrote in 1797, "that the Legislature of this State could see the policy of a gradual Abolition of Slavery."

Strolling today along lanes that lead from the mansion, you come to small white houses equipped for eighteenth-century tasks.

In a roomy kitchen joined to the family dwelling by an arcade, Washington's servants prepared hearty plantation meals. Some of their utensils—pewter warming plates, a bronze skillet, and iron mortar for grinding grain—have found their way back beside the old cooking fireplace. Make-believe chickens brown on spits nearby; artfully imitated beef roasts, cherry pies, and crusty rolls look good enough to eat.

Wheels, winders, flax combs, and wool cards in the spinning house remind us that textiles woven here clothed Mount Vernon's people, with an occasional surplus to sell.

OPPOSITE:
During intervals between more exciting adventures, Washington took great pleasure in the quiet tasks of a gentleman farmer. "I think with you," he wrote a friend in 1788, "that the life of a Husbandman of all others is the most delectable." Throughout the perilous time of the Revolution, he dispatched detailed letters to his Mount Vernon manager, instructing him on what field crops, vegetables, herbs, and fruits to plant; how to care for his livestock, and other essentials of a working farm. When he was home, Washington consulted books and experts on horticulture, and experimented himself with new plants, implements, and methods.

Life of Washington by J. T. Headley. New York Public Library.

Washington cultivated the land surrounding his hilltop mansion in the elaborate style then followed by English country gentlemen. At the same time, he operated his four outlying farms as separate self-contained units. Here, against the steep hill that slopes down from the house toward the estate's wharf, the present tomb (lower left) contains the remains of George and Martha Washington which were transferred from the old family vault in 1831.

Painting by William M. Price circa 1855. New York Public Library

The storehouse displays typical Mount Vernon supplies—seeds, nails, tools; pigments and oil to mix paints; leather to be made into boots and shoes by the cobbler.

Lifelike hams hang in the smokehouse. In the washhouse, wooden tubs recall gossipy scrub sessions. Coachhouse and stable bring back a vanished world of clattering hooves and jouncing wheels on rutted trails.

Though Washington's own carriages have long since crumbled away or been broken up for souvenirs, two contemporary vehicles on view hold close associations.

The curious two-wheeled chair in the coachhouse was driven by Lord Fairfax, patron of Washington's youth. The elegant maroon and gilt-trimmed coach in the stable's carriage compartment belonged to Mayor Samuel Powel of Philadelphia. President and Mrs. Washington probably rode in it with the Powels when Philadelphia was the seat of government.

But Washington seems more natural to us astride a horse. Jefferson called him "the best horseman of his age and the most graceful rider." Walking by the 20 stalls in his handsome brick stable, it is pleasant to recall the spirited saddle horses he kept here and the faithful battle mounts he retired to leisure and plenty of oats.

About a million visitors now roam Mount Vernon in a year. As did Washington's guests, they come by land and water. Those arriving in summer excursion boats dock at the original wharf site.

Few among the swarming crowds realize, however, how much lively work goes on behind the eighteenth-century stage sets.

The present estate, now expanded to nearly 500 acres, covers roughly the area of the old Mansion House Farm. It still raises beef cattle and sheep. Its

early-American gardens are not only for show; they supply flower decoration for the mansion, fresh fruit and vegetables for staff use, and seeds and small potted plants for sale to tourists.

To maintain and exhibit Mount Vernon, the Ladies' Association employs some 100 people compared with Washington's roughly 350 slaves at highest count. Needed now are engineers, carpenters, handymen, cleaning help, and security guards.

The executive staff, headed by a resident director, John A. Castellani, includes professionals in all areas of historic house and museum restoration and preservation.

Accredited researchers allowed to browse among the library's many old books and manuscripts may come on such treasures as a little personal-account book that Washington once carried in his pocket, or one of Martha's rare surviving letters.

To ensure accuracy in restoring buildings, Mount Vernon has had its own architects to see that every detail—from small, irregular bricks to hand-cut cyprus roof shingles—is true to Washington and his period.

Equally important, the twentieth century works for the eighteenth by providing the latest and best devices to protect the old estate. High walls and fences surround the grounds. Searchlights sweep across the lawns at night, and trained watchdogs trot beside guards on rounds.

Structural steel supports the mansion's floors and stairways against the pounding of millions of feet. To prevent fire, only flashlight-carrying watchmen enter after dark. Winter warmth comes from concealed hot-water pipes whose source is 400 feet away in a buried central-heating plant.

Should a flame erupt in the house, automatic fire detectors would find it

At the final resting place of George Washington at Mount Vernon, England's Prince of Wales, later Edward VII, pays his respects to the rebel who made good the separation of the United States from the mother country. Beside the young man stands his host, white-maned President Buchanan. Both before and after Prince Edward's visit in 1860, many other world-famous personages have come here to lay a wreath and praise Washington. But it is the ordinary citizens, pouring through the gates a million strong each year, who help support the institution, and in return see a way of life that is no less real because it has passed.

Painting by Thomas Pritchard. Smithsonian Institution

At the west front of George Washington's old home, President and Mrs. Kennedy entertain guests with a fife-and-drum drill by the Army's 3rd Infantry Old Guard, dressed in Revolution-time uniforms. The occasion was a state dinner, held on July 11, 1961, for President Ayub of Pakistan. The food was prepared in the White House kitchen and transported by truck; the guests, numbering about 135, came by festive yachts. Part of the fun was a menu that might have been offered by Mrs. Washington. The view, from small tables set up on the lawn overlooking the Potomac, was the familiar one long enjoyed by the eighteenth-century residents.

Photograph by Abbie Rowe.
National Archives

out, and built-in chemical-gas sprayers would quickly extinguish it. A mobile fire truck is hidden nearby, and a strategically located system of hooked-up hoses and hydrants stands ready for action at the first whisper of danger. Fire drills are frequent.

Painted by John Trumbull in 1795, these small twin portraits of George and Martha Washington hung in their bedroom during the closing years of their life together.

Lewis Collection, National Museum of American History. Courtesy Smithsonian Institution

George Washington's birthday marks the high point of the year at Mount Vernon. Often the Association's regent and vice regents attend, traveling many miles.

The staff starts the day with a private ceremony of wreath laying at the stone coffin of the General and his lady.

Then, with the measured beat of a funeral march throughout the day, patriotic groups place a rainbow-colored succession of flowers within the tomb's enclosure.

But such ceremonial honors for Washington are not limited to Americans or to a special day. On visits to the United States, kings, queens, and presidents, princes, princesses, and prime ministers take time out to visit and to lay floral tributes at the tomb.

Their signatures color Mount Vernon's guest books with the drama of far places and global events that mark the lives of such famous personages.

Turning the pages at random in these thick guest books, you find, for instance, the flamboyant signature of then reigning Queen Marie of Romania, who, in October 1926, dashed off "Marie" in letters large enough to occupy nearly a quarter of a page.

Haile Selassie, Lion of Judah and King of Kings of Ethiopia, left his name here in 1954, during a fabulous career that had involved exile after Italian invasion of his country in 1935 and his triumphant return to his throne in 1941.

Among other royal visitors, King George VI, Queen Elizabeth, and later their daughter when she was Princess Elizabeth have paid their respects to Washington, the victorious rebel, at his peaceful Virginia home.

On a balmy July night in 1961, Mount Vernon suddenly turned into a fairyland of lights and gaiety. President and Mrs. John F. Kennedy were entertaining Pakistan's President Ayub at a unique state dinner, which had been prepared in the White House, transported, and set up for 135 guests on the lawn beside the Potomac.

Framed by the dark river and the glowing, white-pillared mansion, the diners brought to life a scene of hospitality that gregarious George Washington might well have enjoyed. There was even a fife and drum corps in knee breeches and wigs, who drilled smartly in eighteenth-century style.

Since then, Mount Vernon's guests—royal and otherwise—have continued to represent a gazetteer of places and "Who's Who" of the world.

Prince Charles and his sister, Princess Anne, carried on British tradition in

July 1970, when they toured the estate, after sailing down the Potomac in the Presidential yacht, *Sequoia*.

Members of the Imperial family of Japan arrived separately. Prince Hitachi and his wife came in 1971, following an earlier visit there by Prince and Princess Mikasa; and all of them were eclipsed, in October 1975, by their father, Emperor Hirohito and his wife, Empress Nagako.

Young King Carl Gustaf XVI of Sweden was here in April 1976, and in May of that same year Her Majesty Queen Margrethe and His Royal Highness Prince Henrik of Denmark put in their appearance and signed the waiting guest book.

Between these and other visits by traveling royalty, accompanied by their own retinues, protocol officials, Secret Service men, and the press, have come hundreds of other notables, including a long succession of presidents and military leaders from Latin America and the world.

And for still another category of international visitors, one guest book presents the names of members of three delegations from the People's Republic of China. These visitors from an ancient land were in the United States to discuss petrochemical technology, civil aviation, and trade between the United States and China. Yet they found time to call at the shrine to the hero of what Americans regard as the world's most successful revolution.

But the latest and perhaps the most historically appropriate event at Mount Vernon was a gala dinner held on September 11, 1981. Attended by distinguished French and American guests, it was part of the year's bicentennial celebration of the Franco-American victory over the British at Yorktown. Specifically, it commemorated the dinner given by General Washington 200 years before in honor of his French colleague, General Rochambeau.

That 1781 meeting provided the first occasion during the whole Revolution that had permitted Washington to return to his own home—and then only to host a conference with his officers and French allies on their way to Yorktown.

The eighteenth-century props that embellished Mount Vernon's twentieth-century commemorative dinner included Revolutionary music, uniforms, and regimental flags. Together they helped recreate one of the most significant events of Washington's and the nation's past.

And what would George Washington have thought, we may wonder today, of all the homage paid to him at his beloved estate?

Perhaps the answer to this question lies in his character, his innate modesty and integrity, and in his attitude toward the way of life he would have chosen.

In a letter written in 1790 to his friend and in-law, Dr. David Stuart, he put it this way: "I can truly say I had rather be at Mount Vernon with a friend or two about me than to be attended at the seat of government by the officers of State and the representatives of every power in Europe."

OVERLEAF:
Snow-covered ground and cloudy skies recall a similar scene on December 13, 1799, when Washington left the comfortable warmth of his house to attend to landscaping problems needing attention on his riverside lawn. His exposure to bad weather while marking trees to be cut down doubtless worsened the insipient illness that would cause his death.

Photograph by Thomas Nebbia.
© National Geographic Society

Acknowledgments

FOR A BOOK OF THIS KIND, it would be impossible to give proper thanks for all the help I received from colleagues and others knowledgeable in the field of American history and related subjects. I wish, however, to mention a few of the people and organizations who provided specific information and illustrations material concerning George Washington's life and little-known details involving his remarkable leadership in carrying out the will of Congress in establishing the young Republic's capital by the Potomac:

SILVIO BEDINI, for providing graphic illustrations from his book, *The Life of Benjamin Banneker*.

JEANNE DUIKER, in appreciation for her careful reading of the original manuscript.

RALPH EHRENBERG, Geography and Map Division of the Library of Congress, who furnished valuable information on the first maps of the District of Columbia.

FREDERICKSBURG VISITOR CENTER, for useful data on George Washington's relationships with the city.

ROBERT GOLER, Curator, Fraunces Tavern Museum, for his help in supplying pictorial material.

CORNELIUS HEINE, source of historical research and pictures on the Federal City in Washington's time.

ELIZABETH HULL, with appreciation of her interest and dedication to the chore of indexing.

SIBLEY JENNINGS, whose long research on the architectural career of L'Enfant shed new light on the genius of the man who designed America's permanent capital.

JUNIOR LEAGUE OF WASHINGTON, whose staff for *The City of Washington* gave helpful material on text and illustrations used in this George Washington book.

JOHN KILBOURNE, Director of Anderson House Museum, Society of the Cincinnati, for illustrative and supporting material on Washington and the Society.

MARGARET KLAPTHOR, Curator of Political History, Smithsonian Institution, for contributing important picture material.

JANE LINGO, administrative staff of George Washington University, for her cooperation in supplying original research material for illustrations.

ARTHUR MILLER, National Park Service, Mid-Atlantic Region, who made available the latest information on research at Washington's birthplace.

EARL MINDERMAN, for the use of his paintings of Forrest-Marbury House and Rhodes Tavern, and for the research that helped document their historic significance.

BETTY MONKMAN, White House Curator's Office, for rare background on the laying of the White House cornerstone.

MOUNT VERNON LADIES' ASSOCIATION OF THE UNION, whose staff answered numerous questions, and whose curator, Christine Meadows, reviewed the book's Mount Vernon section to check on recent changes.

NATIONAL CAPITAL REGION OF THE NATIONAL PARK SERVICE, for information and illustrative material by these staff members: Historian Gary Scott, Don Heilemann and Bill Clark of Photographic Service.

FORREST WAYNE POWARS, for his generous and enthusiastic support of the book in all its ideological and practical aspects.

JON REYNOLDS, Archivist, Georgetown University, for useful information concerning Washington's interest in promoting higher education for young Americans.

NELSON RIMENSNYDER, Historian for the House District Committee of the U.S. Congress, who provided key advice on the founding of the Nation's permanent capital.

FRED SCHWENGEL, president of the U.S. Capitol Historical Society, whose interest in American history and George Washington encouraged the production of this book.

WILLIAM A. SMITH, for the use of his painting on the first surveys made of the District of Columbia.

FLORIAN THAYN, Office of the Architect of the Capitol, who came up with ready and knowledgeable answers to any and all questions regarding the Capitol and related subjects.

DAVID WHITE, Museum director of the Connecticut State Library at Hartford, for his prompt and generous cooperation in supplying illustration material.

Selected Bibliography

Andrist, Ralph K., editor. *The Founding Fathers: George Washington, A Biography in His Own Words*, vols. 1 and 2. Newsweek Book Division, New York. 1972.

Architect of the Capitol. *Art in the United States Capitol*. United States Government Printing Office, Washington, D.C. 1976.

Ashworth, Mary Wells. *See* Caroll, John Alexander.

Bacheler, Irving, and Kates, Herbert S. *Great Moments in the Life of Washington*. Grosset & Dunlap, Publishers, New York. 1932.

Baker, Marcus. "Surveys and Maps of the District of Columbia." *The National Geographic Magazine*, November 1894. The National Geographic Society, Washington, D.C.

Bedini, Silvio A. "Benjamin Banneker and the Survey of the District of Columbia," *Records of the Columbia Historical Society of Washington*. Columbia Historical Society, Washington, D.C. 1969-70.

——————————. *The Life of Benjamin Banneker*. Charles Scribner's Sons, New York. 1972.

Beinke, Nancy K., editor. *Historic American Buildings Survey: District of Columbia Catalog*. National Park Service, Washington, D.C. 1968.

Bryan, Wilhelmus Bogart. *A History of the National Capital: From Its Foundation Through the Period of the Adoption of the Organic Act*, vol. 1, 1790-1814. The Macmillan Company, New York. 1914.

Bryant, William Cullen, and Gay, Sydney Howard. *A Popular History of the United States . . .*, vol. III. Charles Scribner's Sons, New York. 1879.

Caemmerer, H. Paul. *The Life of Pierre Charles L'Enfant, Planner of the City Beautiful: The City of Washington*. National Republic Publishing Company, Washington, D.C. 1950.

Carroll, John Alexander, and Ashworth, Mary Wells. *George Washington*, vol. 7. (Completing the biography by Douglas Southall Freeman.) Charles Scribner's Sons, New York. 1957.

Clark, Allen C. *Greenleaf and Law in The Federal City*. Press of W. F. Roberts, Washington, D.C. 1901.

Columbia Historical Society, *Records* of the, Washington, D.C. Vols. 2 (1889), 4 (1901), 17 (1914), 20 (1917), containing letters of George Washington, and other material concerning the surveying, planning, and development of the National Capital.

Cowdrey, Albert E. *A City for the Nation. The Army Engineers and the Building of Washington, 1790-1967*. U.S. Government Printing Office, Washington, D.C. 1979.

Cox, William V., compiler. Celebration of the One Hundredth Anniversary of the Establishment of the Seat of Government in the District of Columbia. Government Printing Office, Washington, D.C. 1901.

Cunliffe, Marcus. *George Washington: Man and Monument.* Little, Brown and Company, Boston. 1958.

——————————. *George Washington and the Making of a Nation.* American Heritage Publishing Co., Inc., New York. 1966.

Custis, George Washington Parke. *Recollections and Private Memoirs of Washington . . .* Bradley and Company, Philadelphia. 1867.

Davis, Deering; Dorsey, Stephen P.; Hall, Ralph Cole. *Georgetown Houses of the Federal Period, Washington, D.C., 1780-1830.* Architectural Book Publishing Co., Inc., New York. 1944.

Dictionary of American Biography. Charles Scribner's Sons, New York. 1929 —.

Dorsay, Stephen P. *See* Davis, Deering.

Durant, John and Alice. *Pictorial History of American Presidents.* A. S. Barnes and Company, New York. 1955.

Ehrenberg, Ralph E. "Mapping the Nation's Capital, The Surveyor's Office, 1791-1818," *The Quarterly Journal of the Library of Congress,* vol. 36, no. 3, summer 1979.

Encyclopedia Britannica, 9th edition. William Benton, Publisher, Chicago. 1967.

Federal Writers' Project, Works Progress Administration. *Washington, City and Capital.* American Guide Series. United States Government Printing Office, Washington, D.C. 1937.

Felder, Paula S., editor. *George Washington's Relations and Relationships in Fredericksburg, Virginia.* Historic Publications of Fredericksburg, Fredericksburg, Virginia. 1981.

Fitzpatrick, John C., editor. *The Diaries of George Washington 1748-1799,* 4 volumes. Houghton Mifflin Company, Boston and New York. 1925.

——————————. *The Writings of George Washington from the Original Manuscript Sources, 1745-1799,* vol. 31. (Prepared under the direction of the U.S. George Washington Bicentennial Commission.) U.S. Government Printing Office, Washington, D.C. 1939.

Flexner, James Thomas. *George Washington: The Forge of Experience (1732-1775).* Little, Brown and Company, Boston. 1965.

——————————. *George Washington in the American Revolution (1775-1783).* Little, Brown and Company, Boston. 1968.

——————————. *George Washington: Anguish and Farewell (1793-1799).* Little, Brown and Company, Boston. 1972.

——————————. *George Washington and the New Nation (1783-1793).* Little, Brown and Company, Boston. 1970.

Ford, Paul Leicester. *The True George Washington.* J. B. Lippincott Company, Philadelphia. 1896.

Frary, I. T. *They Built The Capitol.* Garrett and Massie, Incorporated, Richmond, Virginia. 1940.

Freeman, Douglas Southall. *George Washington: A Biography,* vols. 1-6. (Vol. 7, *see* J. A. Carroll and M. W. Ashworth.) Charles Scribner's Sons, New York, New York. 1948-1954.

Freidel, Frank. *Our Country's Presidents.* National Geographic Society, Washington, D.C. Eighth Edition, 1981.

Frost, John. *Pictorial Life of George Washington . . .* Leary, Getz & Co., Philadelphia. 1860.

Garraty, John Arthur. *The American Nation: A History of the United States,* Fourth edition. Harper and Row, New York. 1979.

Gay, Sydney. *See* Bryant, William Cullen.

Green, Constance McLaughlin. *Washington: Village and Capital, 1800-1878.* Princeton University Press, Princeton, New Jersey. 1962.

Hall, Ralph Cole. *See* Davis, Deering.

Harper's New Monthly Magazine. Harper & Brothers, Publishers, New York. "George Washington," by John S. C. Abbott. Vol. 12, February 1856.
"Mount Vernon As It Is." Vol. 18, March 1859.
"The English Home of the Washingtons." Vol. 58, March 1879.
"Washington as a Burgher." Vol. 60, February 1880.
"The First American: His Homes and His Households," by Leila Herbert. Vol. 99, September-November 1899.

Hines, Christian. *Early Recollections of Washington City* [Reprint of September 1866 edition]. Junior League of Washington. Washington, D.C. 1981.

Hirst, Francis W. *Life and Letters of Thomas Jefferson.* The Macmillan Company, New York. 1926.

Jennings, J. L. Sibley, Jr. "Artistry As Design, L'Enfant's Extraordinary City," *The Quarterly Journal of the Library of Congress,* vol. 36, no. 3, summer 1979.

Johnston, Jay. "Waterway to Washington, the C & O Canal," *The National Geographic Magazine,* vol. 117, no. 3, March 1960. The National Geographic Society, Washington, D.C.

Junor League of Washington. *The City of Washington. An Illustrated History,* Thomas Froncek, editor. Alfred A. Knopf, New York. 1977.

Ketchum, Richard M. *The World of George Washington.* American Heritage Publishing Company, Inc., New York. 1974.

Kinnaird, Clark. *George Washington, The Pictorial Biography.* Hastings House, Publishers, Inc., New York. 1967.

Kite, Elizabeth S. *L'Enfant and Washington 1791-1792. Published and Unpublished Documents Now Brought Together for the First Time. Historical Documents, Institut Français de Washington, Cahier III.* The Johns Hopkins Press, Baltimore. 1929.

LePhillips, Phillip. "The Negro, Benjamin Banneker; Astronomer and Mathematician, Plea for Universal Peace," *Records of the Columbia Historical Society,* vol. 20, 1917.

Lossing, Benson J. *Life of Washington; A Biography—Personal, Military, and Political,* 3 vols. Virtue and Company, New York. 1860.

——————. *Mary and Martha; The Mother and the Wife of George Washington.* Harper and Brothers, Franklin Square, New York. 1886.

——————. *Mount Vernon and Its Associations, Historical, Biographical, and Pictorial.* W. A. Townsend & Company, New York. 1859.

——————. *Our Country, A Household History . . . ,* vols., 1 and 2. Johnson & Miles, New York. 1877.

——————. *The Pictorial Field-Book of the Revolution,* vols. I and II. Harper and Brothers, New York. 1860.

Loth, David. *Alexander Hamilton, Portrait of a Prodigy.* Carrick and Evans, Inc., New York. 1939.

MacDonald, William. *George Washington, A Brief Biography.* The Mount Vernon Ladies' Association of the Union. Mount Vernon, Virginia. 1973.

Mackall, S. Somervell. *Early Days of Washington.* The Neale Company, Washington, D.C. 1899.

Malone, Dumas. *Jefferson and the Rights of Man.* Little, Brown and Company, Boston. 1951.

Mathews, Catherine Van Cortlandt. *Andrew Ellicott, His Life and Letters.* The Grafton Press, New York. 1908.

McDonald, Forrest. *The Presidency of George Washington.* The University Press of Kansas. Lawrence/Manhattan/Wichita. 1973.

McDowell, Bart. *The Revolutionary War, America's Fight for Freedom.* National Geographic Society, Washington, D.C. 1967.

Michael, William H. *The Declaration of Independence: Illustrated Story of Its Adoption with the Biographies and Portraits of the Signers and of the Secretary of the Congress.* Government Printing Office, Washington, D.C. 1904.

Moore, Charles. *The Family Life of George Washington.* Houghton, Boston. 1926.

Mount Vernon, An Illustrated Handbook. The Mount Vernon Ladies' Association of the Union, Mount Vernon, Virginia. 1974.

Newsweek, editors of *The Founding Fathers: Thomas Jefferson, A Biography in His Own Words,* vol. 2. Newsweek, New York. 1972.

Nicolay, Helen. *Our Capitol on the Potomac.* The Century Company, New York, London. 1924.

Padover, Saul K., editor. *Thomas Jefferson and the National Capitol . . . 1783-1818.* Government Printing Office, Washington, D.C. 1946.

Proctor, John Clagett. *Proctor's Washington and Environs.* Written for the Washington Sunday Star. 1928-1949.

Putnam's Monthly. "Washington's Early Days." Vol. 3, January 1854.

Ridpath, John Clark. *People's History of the United States.* Greencastle, Indiana. 1895.

Rivoire, Mario. *The Life and Times of Washington . . . ,* Orlandi, Enzo, general editor; C. J. Richards, translator. Arnoldo Mondadori Editore and the Curtis Publishing Company, Philadelphia and New York. 1965.

Roberts, Chalmers McGeagh. *Washington Past and Present; A Pictorial History of the Nation's Capital.* Public Affairs Press, Washington, D.C. 1950.

Sawyer, Joseph Dillaway. *Washington,* 2 vols. The Macmillan Company, New York. 1927.

Schachner, Nathan. *Thomas Jefferson, A Biography,* vol. I. Appleton-Century-Crofts, Inc., New York. 1951.

Schroeder, John Frederick. *Life and Times of Washington . . . ,* vols. I and II. Johnson, Fry, and Company, New York. 1857.

Showalter, William Joseph. "The Travels of George Washington," *The National Geographic Magazine,* vol. 61, no. 1, January 1932. The National Geographic Society, Washington, D.C.

Smith, Page. *Jefferson, A Revealing Biography.* American Heritage Publishing Co., Inc., New York. 1976.

Somerville, Mollie. *Washington Walked Here. Alexandria on the Potomac: One of America's First "New" Towns.* Colortone Press, Washington, D.C. 1970.

Stephenson, Richard W. "The Delineation of a Grand Plan," *The Quarterly Journal of the Library of Congress,* vol. 36, no. 3, summer 1979.

Thane, Elswyth. *Potomac Squire.* Duell, Sloan and Pearce, New York. 1963.

Tindall, William. *Standard History of the City of Washington from a Study of the Original Sources.* H. W. Crew and Company, Knoxville, Tennessee. 1914.

United States George Washington Bicentennial Commission. *Activities of the Commission and Complete—Final Report of the United States George Washington Bicentennial Commission,* vols. I-V. United States George Washington Bicentennial Commission, Washington, D.C. 1932.

Van Doren, Carl (introduced by). *The Patriotic Anthology.* Doubleday, Doran and Company, Inc., Garden City, New York. 1941.

Wall, Charles Cecil. *George Washington, Citizen-Soldier.* University Press of Virginia, Charlottesville, Virginia. 1980.

Wilson, Woodrow. *A History of the American People,* vols. I and II. Harper and Brothers Publishers, New York, London. 1906.

Woodward, Fred E. "A Ramble Along the Boundary Stones of the District of Columbia With a Camera," *Records of the Columbia Historical Society,* vol. 20, 1917.

Index

Page numbers in italic refer to illustrations.

OTHER BOOKS BY LONNELLE AIKMAN

We, the People: The Story of the United States Capitol. Prepared for the United States Capitol Historical Society by the National Geographic Society. Washington, D.C. From the first edition (1963), through the twelfth (1981).

G. Washington, Man and Monument. Prepared for the Washington National Monument Association by the National Geographic Society. Washington, D.C. 1965, 1973. Coauthor Frank Freidel, Harvard Professor of History.

The Living White House. Prepared for the White House Historical Association by the National Geographic Society. Washington, D.C. From the first edition (1966), through the seventh (1982).

Nature's Healing Arts: From Folk Medicine to Modern Drugs. Special Publications Division, National Geographic Society. Washington, D.C. 1977.

Designed by Gerard A. Valerio, Bookmark Studio

Composed in Goudy Linotype by Service Composition,
Baltimore, Maryland

Printed on Mohawk Superfine by Collins Lithography,
Baltimore, Maryland

Bound in Strathmore Beau Brilliant and Joanna Devon
by A. Horowitz & Sons, Fairfield, New Jersey